The Speaker's Notes

Words that changed my life forever

Managing Editor
Scott P. Dawson

Contents

LEXI

SCOTT

Acknowledgements

Introduction

The Speaker's Notes is a book that was designed to share different real life struggles we all go through and how we've gotten through them. There is no one way to overcome trials but having someone share their way can help you become closer to reaching your break through. In this book you'll experience deep pains, struggles, and triumphs with each author while taking you through a shared period of their life. The point is to let you know that you're never alone and someone has been where you are but did not stay there. We share our stories to give you hope and inspire you to reach a new height with tools learned through personal experience. Our prayers are that we are able to reach you where you are and help give you some tools to help you along your life's journey.

KATIE

Born and raised in Evansville Indiana, Katie Johnson is one of 5 children raised by a single parent. Life's challenges of homelessness, poverty and sexual abuse did not stop her from hurdling any obstacle in her way, literally and figuratively.

Katie graduated from William Henry Harrison High School with a full track and field scholarship to Ball State University, where she continued to break athletic records and academic barriers as a first generation college student in her family. She received her Bachelor of Science in Communication Studies and studied abroad in Australia and South Africa.

Katie believes that life is not about focusing on the negative of what one has been through, but finding the positive in any and every situation. As an educator in an urban charter school, a life coach, a mentor and a motivational speaker, her mission is to help people live fully and freely into the best chapter of their lives. Her experiences with Teach for America, HerSpace Inc., Big Brother Big Sister, KIPP Schools and Zarvos Leadership and Coaching have demonstrated her commitment to inspiring and touching the lives of others.

As the founder of KLJohnson Motivates, LLC she brings her passion, energy and authenticity to help audiences and groups see beyond their today into their tomorrow. This is no career for Katie; this is her calling.

Chapter 1

My Introduction to Forgiveness

My mother loved to read, so I guess that explains why I love to read so much. Books allowed my mom to escape her reality of being a single parent of 4 with 3 different men, no high school diploma and being in an unfulfilling and unhealthy relationship with my dad. Books allow people to see life through another person's perspective, escape realities and sometimes, use their imagination to create new worlds. I guess that's what my mother was doing the day before I was born. I always wanted to be a time traveler, so let me paint you a picture:

> *On June 22nd 1987, my mother was sitting on her bed doing what she loved to do: reading. (I'm sure it was some romance novel with that tall cute white man who has the long flowing hair and painted on abs and some body of water looking refreshingly welcoming, but I digress...) By the age of 20, my mother had 4 children - my oldest brother James (Mann), my twin brothers Stephan and Kevin and her youngest at the time Demetrice (Meady) - and had one on the way. My original due date was the 26th, but on that day when she was enjoying her favorite hobby, the boys were busy getting into trouble. As told by my mother, while reading she heard this loud WOOOSH and then smelled fire. Somehow, some way, my brothers and uncle had gotten a hold of a lighter and caught my mother's closet, full of clothes, on fire. My mother jumped up - 8 month old belly and all - ran to the closet and began stomping on clothes and pulling kids out one by one. As you can imagine the stress from seeing 4 young boys in the back of a burning closet can make anyone go into shock, but instead, my mom went into labor.*

Born and raised in Evansville Indiana, I was one of 5 children. More specifically, I was my mother's last child and only girl. Growing up with four older brothers was rough at times, and they always tried to steal my food if I didn't eat fast enough. Depending on the day, one of them would be picking on me, and as a result, being a tomboy came naturally. But, there were plenty advantages too: I learned to fight, I learned what pure and unconditional love is and I also learned that someone always had my back. When things went wrong as a kid, and they often did, my brothers and I learned how to stick up for one another and be a team. If one person got in trouble, we all got in trouble; they taught me loyalty.

One time, two of my brothers were play-fighting and broke my mom's lamp in the living room while she was at work, which was all the time. We knew that whoever did it was going to get a whopping, so we decided that we were not going to tell on each other. When my mom got home, she called everyone into the living room and asked who did it. No one said a word, and yes, we all got in trouble; but we stood together and created an even stronger bond after that. I trusted them and I knew that they would never let anything happen to me. And, based on what they knew, they did just that. I was surrounded by males who loved me and a mom that worked countless hours to provide for her family.

The older I get, the more I respect my mother for the sacrifices she made to take care of my brothers and I. While my father was around, he was not always the nicest to my mom. Actually, most of the interactions that I can remember between the two of them were pretty volatile. Though he was not a nice man to my mom, I was still a daddy's girl.

A lot of my friends didn't have their fathers around and I just knew that my father loved me. I can remember some of the things he would say while tucking me into bed. Things like, "You are daddy's girl and you know daddy loves you so much". I would ask, "How much?" and he would say, "Until the moon turned blue" or "Until the sky turned purple". I wish I would have known then that on some stormy days/nights a beautiful blue sky can turn dark blue and almost purple, or that there is such a thing a blue moon that happens every 2-3 years. If I had known those things, I would have known that his love wasn't as rare as he made it seem.

They say that a little girl's father is the first man she will ever love and my father was, but he was also the first man to hurt me, cheat me and cause me pain. They also say that most times that girls will date or marry a man like her father. Well, I chose a different path because if that were true, I would have dated men that were both physically and sexually abusive and those who were bad decision makers. I remember when my world changed: when my beautiful blue sky of a relationship with my father actually turned into that deep, dark, scary purple.

> *I was at my best friend's house, and while playing in her room - more like prank calling some of our other friends - we overheard her older sister and her boyfriend having sex. We quickly stopped making calls and focused our attention on the "ohhs", the "ahhhs" and the panting from her bedroom. We snuck out into the wooden hallway and took turns peeking into the small peephole to see them in action, and to get a better understanding of the sounds that were coming from behind the closed door.*
> *To this day, I'm not sure why my friend and I were taking a bath together at such and old age, but during our bath, her sister came in and we began to ask her questions about what she and her boyfriend were doing. Brandi answered and explained many things about sex and relationships. Then, as casually, and as*

4

calm, as reading a boring text in class, I said to Autumn and Brandi, "My dad does that to me".

As an adult, I can only imagine the fear, anger and disbelief that her older sister must have experienced in that moment: a 10-year-old girl just revealed that her father has had sex with her and she was not afraid or ashamed to admit it. I was so cavalier with my revelation because, at the time, I didn't know that it was wrong; I was just daddy's little girl. Brandi asked me to repeat what I said, so I did. She panicked and told me to get dressed and go home and tell my mom exactly what I told her and that if I did not then she would come down to my house later to talk to my mom. In that moment, I knew something was wrong, but my mind was not capable of understanding the magnitude of my innocent confession.

I found myself running back to my house, which was about a half block from Autumn's. I approached our corner home, took the stairs two at a time and yelled for my mom. I found her in her room doing what she loved to do…you guessed it: reading. I sat on her bed and, once again, casually regurgitated what I had just seen, and what I told Autumn and Brandi. After seeing my mom's face, I knew that something was wrong. My mom gazed into my eyes and her tears started to flow. She wrapped her body around me as if she was trying to shield me from something harmful coming at us full speed. What she was trying to shield her only daughter from, was the pain that I would experience as I lived and dealt with the aftermath of abuse: a lack of self-worth, promiscuity, a lack of trust for men, several years of nightmares waking me out of my sleep and being fearful that the man that had taken my innocence would hurt me again.

What I didn't know about my situation was that I had painted my father as this larger than life *Monster*. And, for those who like scary movies, you know that when we fear the monster, the more power it has and the less power we have over it; and that is exactly what happened. Every time I had a nightmare, it would wake me out of my sleep. I remember several times while I was dating my college boyfriend, I experienced a recurring dream of my father, who is only 5 feet 8 inches, turning into a large villain chasing me through the streets of my neighborhood address and sometimes my college campus, which he had never visited. I would go from running for my life in my dreams to literally jumping out of my sleep in a cold sweat. I even woke up my boyfriend at the time and asked him to tell me who he was because I feared that the body next to mine was the Monster's. He had the power.

However, after almost 20 years since I shared my abuse with my mom, I am finally free from my Monster and I now have the power over my situation and over my life. I am not saying that I no longer feel sad, feel angry, or that I don't think about my past, but I decided and am committed to not letting my abuse control my life and happiness, which is what it had done for years. As I said before, when we hang on to things from the past - hurt, shame, fear and the experiences that causes those emotions - we are giving that experience, or that person, our power. In most cases we are unable to differentiate whether the decisions that we make, or actions that we take are our fault entirely or not.

For example, due to my abuse, I have been extremely aware of the type of men that I date, which is a great thing. I have learned to set my standards, and if a nice guy is interested in me, he knows where I stand concerning how I want to be treated and what I expect from our relationship. In contrast, I have also experienced fear when thinking about the relationship between my future husband and my daughter. I cannot wait to see her crawl into his arms and look at him as if he is superman; I desire to see him put his brief case down after a long day of work and be immediately rejuvenated just by her smile, and I cannot wait for him to take her on her first date to show her how a respectful gentleman should treat a lady.

But, in the midst of wanting all those things for my future daughter, I know that my personal damage may ruin some of those amazing images: like an innocent daddy daughter kiss will make me remember that my dad and I shared many kisses when his intentions were ill. Or, if they have cute little sayings like "I love you until the moon turns blue or the sky turns purple", that will be a trigger and take me back to my 10-year-old self. Or, if I see her sitting on his lap, I may have to push aside a disturbing thought that there could be something ill and malicious also taking place. That is power. Those thoughts have consumed me for years, and while I am happy to say that I am in a much better place than before, I still have so much growth to do.

As I think about the growth that I have experienced, there are a few choices that I have made that were absolutely necessary:

1. I admitted to myself that I needed therapy and sought out professional help.
2. I learned to accept that my abuse happened and allowed myself to feel the emotions of having "a moment".
3. I forgave him with no action required from him; no admission on his part, no apology on his part and no future relationship required… (I'm still on this journey so I'm not quite ready for that yet).

By taking these steps I was able to learn so much about myself and how my abuse had, and still is affecting my life. There are many people that have this idea that once someone forgives a person, or gets help, that the pain goes away or that they are "healed". I highly discourage people from having this mindset because it couldn't be more false. The pain from being abused, or going through any type of traumatic experience, does not go away automatically or easily. When I reflect on why I still think about my abuse, or the hurt of what happened, I use the analogy of having a scar.

> When I was in the 4th grade, my brother and I were "neighbors" in that our bedrooms were right beside each other. There was actually a small window that was in the middle of the wall that separated us, so we used this window to talk to each other, pass snacks and harass each other. One morning, my brother decided to wake me up by using the window as drum, and his knuckles as his drum sticks. He tapped on the window for at least five minutes before I asked him -I'm sure not so nicely - to stop (When you live in a house with 4 other siblings, there is always a system for who gets up first and who gets a little extra sleep). On this particular day, my mom and I had worked out a plan: because I was up late getting my hair braided the night before, my mom said that I could get up later that morning so that I could have a few more minutes of sleep. I guess that message wasn't communicated to my brother

because he just kept tapping on my window. And, after saying stop more times than I can remember, I punched the glass window with all my might, hoping to make him stop; the result was that I had to get 3 stitches on my left arm.

My mother must not have had the best insurance because my stitch job was not very good. Even after 20 years, my scar is still very visible. Most times I don't think about it, but I know it's there and I remember how it happened; I just life live not thinking about it. But, every once in a while, I graze it against something, or someone grabs my arm without knowing about the scar and it tingles or I can feel pain just below the surface of my scars.

This is how most victims (or victors) of abuse are. Most days we don't think about our past, or the person that caused us so much pain, and we are just fine. But every so often, there is something that triggers the pain of our past. Maybe there was a movie on TV where someone was abused; or maybe someone told a joke. Maybe they ran into the person that hurt them, and that pain that was lying dormant for so many years resurfaces and hits them like a ton of bricks and they have "A Moment". Part of the healing process is allowing those moments to happen and not ignoring them because no matter what, the scar will always be there, but you also get to decide how much you want to feel the pain of you past; Forgiveness allows you to push through the pain of your past and prepare for a brighter future.

End of chapter reflections

Chapter 1: Think about it
- Who in your past or present do you feel like you want/need to forgive? Why?
- What events in your life have you given your power to?
- How do you currently cope with issues that arise from your past?

Chapter 1: Take Action
- Get a journal and write down the things, people events that are triggers in your life.
- Write down your reactions to the triggers: what do you do when you experience a trigger, who do you reach out to and what are the steps you usually take after dealing with a trigger.

Chapter 2

Understanding The Importance of Forgiveness

When the bell rang for recess, that signified my favorite part of the school day, and I would run outside to get in line for one of my favorite competitions. When I was younger I was the queen of tug-of-war in my middle school. I would wrap the rope around my hands and lean back for the win; I always liked it better when we played outside versus inside because I could dig my feet into the ground and have more grip to beat my opponent. The joy I experienced after winning was amazing. I would have to say that the only feeling I enjoyed more than pulling my opponent across the line and winning, was letting go of the heavy rope that had caused my hands to swell up and bruise.

The feeling of letting go was amazing; Not only does letting go feel good, but it's also important and necessary. Had I not let go of the ropes that were wrapped around my hands, I would not have been able to attend my next class, or go to eat lunch, so I had to let go. And, just like I had to let of the rope during recess, I had to let go of the past hurt from my abuse.

Any time we experience traumatic situations, there is always something that we are hanging on to, or that is hanging on to us. During the healing process we have to ask ourselves, *what are we hanging on to? What is making us want to continue to give the person or situation power? And Why?* Many times we do not want to let go, or forgive. Most times we hang on, or refuse to forgive so that we have an excuse or someone to blame if things do not go as we think they should.

Many young women that have been abused physically, sexually or emotionally, have admitted to being sexually active at an early age and having had several sexual partners. I recently spoke with a past student of mine - a teen mom - who had been sexually abused by a close family member. I asked her why she believed she became sexually active so early, and she expressed that because she was abused, she didn't value herself or her body. So, when one of her male friends wanted to have sex, she didn't see anything wrong with it. While she may not have valued herself or her body, she was also operating and living a life based on an excuse: the excuse that being abused meant that she didn't have to value herself. The sooner we identify what excuses we are allowing to run our lives, the sooner we are able to deal with our excuses, which allows us to forgive ourselves and the people that caused us pain.

The importance of forgiving is understanding that once we forgive and let go of the situation, we then have to take responsibility of everything that happens from that moment forth. We have to own our mistakes and shortcomings and yes, they may be directly connected to a previous situation or traumatic experience. However, once we forgive, we now have the power and, from there, we can begin to understand why we do the things we do.

Understanding how our previous experiences have shaped our actions and life is a large task. In the previous chapter, I mentioned that during my journey of healing and growth, there were three choices that were absolutely necessary:

1. I admitted to myself that I needed therapy and sought out professional help.
2. I learned to accept that my abuse happened and allowed myself to feel the emotions of having "a moment".
3. I forgave my abuser with no action required from him: no admission on his part, no apology on his part and no future relationship required (I'm still on this journey so I'm not quite ready for that just yet.)

When thinking about the importance of forgiving and letting go so that healing, ownership and responsibility can take place, professional help is extremely important. As a young Black woman, I grew up in a community that did not welcome "outside help" (i.e. therapists). My family and friends all thought that therapists were for *crazies* and *rich white people*; they also lived by the "what happens in this house stays in the house" rule. I will say though, that that rule did not stand when my mother found out my father had sexually abused me; she called the police, and informed my other family members of what happened to help protect me.

I only remember talking to a therapist relatively soon after the abuse was brought to light, but not continuing the sessions after the smoke had cleared. As a college student, when the nightmares resurfaced and the unworthiness snuck back into my life, I used the free counseling services on campus. Even then, after I thought I was "healed" I stopped going. If only I had known then, that healing is a life long journey, I would have continued seeing my therapist instead of waiting for a crisis or a "moment" to happen.

A "moment" happened when I was out once, celebrating a friend's birthday and had way too much to drink. Initially, I wanted to drive home, but my friends refused to give me my keys. I am grateful for their persistence now, but at the time, it was infuriating: It was my car, that I paid for, that was in my name, but they refused to let me drive it. They had taken my control to leave and get out of that situation, but after talking more with them, I knew I could not drive home so I left the party and sat in my parked car. After a while, many of my friends became worried and decided to check in on me; one of those people was my ex-boyfriend.

He and I were not close friends any longer, but we still cared for each other. I knew he still cared and wanted to make sure I was safe because he refused to leave me in my car alone in the middle of the night. Frustrated, I left my car and began to walk down by the canal.

> *As you can imagine, an intoxicated woman walking down by a canal after midnight could be a Lifetime movie waiting to happen, so my ex-boyfriend continued to walk behind me to make sure I was safe. I yelled*

at him, telling him to leave me alone and go back to the party, but he refused. Once again, I felt as if I had no control over the situation and that angered me. I then turned around from walking and charged at him. After spitting out too many vulgar words to count, I balled up my fist, wound up my arm and punched him in his chest.

At the time, I did not make the connection that my lack of control is what had pushed me over the edge. As a child, I had no control over how my father abused my mother, I had no control over not understanding the relationship between my father and I, and I had no control over my innocence being taking away for my father.

So on that night, by the canal, the lack of control to have my keys, to leave and to be left alone, caused me to hurt someone that I truly loved and for me; that was unacceptable. I knew that it would take more than my *want*, to not want to hit someone again; it would take more than understanding that violence is wrong, because I already knew those things. I knew that I hated the feeling of watching someone being abused but, in that moment, when I hit him, none of that mattered. In that moment, that was the only way I felt that I was able to get my point across. In that moment, to me, my violence was justified. But, after that moment, I realized that I knew better and it scared me. I questioned myself, "Was I always meant to be an abuser? Would this be how I will treat the man that I choose to marry and start a family with?" Because I knew what I wanted those answers to be, but couldn't guarantee it, I knew I needed the assistance of someone else to deal with this; I knew I needed to go back to therapy.

At that moment, the urgency to go back to counseling was so great that the following business day, I was on the phone setting up a counseling session. I felt so guilty because one of the things that I hated about my dad was that he abused my mom. He hurt her and my brothers many times and I was there witnesses to his violent moments.

On that night on the canal, my anger got the best of me and I physically hurt someone that I loved. In that moment, I turned into the *Monster*. I became the abuser, and after that moment, I vowed to go back to counseling, even though counseling or participating in any therapy is not an easy journey.

As a past college athlete, I think about the times whenever I had a cramp or sore muscle. While running track, I dealt with several strained hamstring and quad muscles. Our athletic trainer would either use his hands to give me a deep tissue massage and rub out any knots, or use a tool that reminds me of a rolling pin to apply pressure to the knots and roll them out. No matter what method he used, there was always pain when helping to remove the knots and cramps from my legs. After the rolling, or massages though, I always felt better and was able to have a productive practice.

This is how many of my counseling sessions went: it always hurt when getting the 'knots out'. When dealing with a painful past, there are things that we try to forget about, hide from ourselves, or suppress and actually forget that it happened. When in counseling, we are faced with the challenge, and are given the opportunity to unclutter all of those things. And, in the process of decluttering and cleaning out, we come across things that we may not have wanted to face or talk about. In those moments, the knots of our past have to be rubbed out so that we can move on and deal with how that knot affects our lives.

So I ask you, what knots are you refusing to get rubbed out? What situations in your past are cramping your actions, your decisions and your life? The truth is, every decision that we make and every action that we take comes from somewhere and, the sooner we figure out what drives our decision making, the sooner we are able to take control. We then will have the ability to clear out the things that have caused us pain.

Going to therapy was one of the best decisions I have ever made. I am confident that my therapist helped me through moments in my life that had the potential to break my spirit and self-confidence. Because she equipped me with the tools that I needed to handle the situations, I came out a better person. My therapist was understanding, but held me accountable. She was patient, but refused to let me cheat myself by hiding from my past. She was calm in the mist of me having major melt downs, and she made me own my decisions and mistakes while helping me find the root of my decision making and issues.

Finding the right therapist will take time. I must say that it can be intimidating if you have never visited a therapist, or have never had any counseling before. My first suggestion would be to ask if any of your friends, or family know of a good therapist and get references from them. Although it may be a new experience for some, it is worth it.

End of chapter reflections

Chapter 2: Think about it
- What actions in your life have you blamed your traumatic event for?
- What excuses do you get to make due to holding on to past hurts or events in your life?

Chapter 2: Take Action
- In your journal, call yourself out when you find yourself using your past hurts or events, and ask what is the real reason behind your actions.

Chapter 3

The Power of forgiveness

According to RAINN (Rape, Abuse & Incest National Network), out of the yearly 63,000 sexual abuse cases substantiated or corroborated by Child Protective Services (CPS),[6] the perpetrator was most often the parent.[1] That is a staggering number, 80% of perpetrators are parents. 80% of innocent young boys and girls are taken advantage of by someone they trust. 80% of little girls and boys are violated by someone within the home. 80% have to deal with questions like, "What did I do to deserve this?" and, in many cases, they also have to deal with the internal conflict of wanting that perpetrator to continue loving them, or wishing and praying that that person had genuinely loved them enough not to hurt them. Though 80% are abused by a parent, 100% of all sexually abused children have to deal with the aftermath of their abuse. As children, the ability to understand the magnitude of sexual abuse is almost impossible, especially when they are a part of that 80%. Being a VICTOR (not victim) of sexual abuse is a journey that I take stride towards everyday.

The feeling of *true forgiveness* is one that I doubt has been expressed fully in my life. I've never been into super heroes, but in December of 2015, I felt like one. For years when I woke up on Christmas mornings, I was eager to open presents; not that year. That year, I woke up with an unwavering desire to find and forgive my father - a man that I had not seen or spoken to in years. Even though the city that I grew up is the 3rd largest city in Indiana, it is not hard to find someone if you are looking for them, and on that day, I was on a mission to find my father. I located one of my aunt's numbers and called her to see if he would be there. She told me yes, and said that I was welcomed to stop by. My brother seemed nervous about me going to talk to him, so as I left my grandmother's house to head to my aunt's home, he jumped into my car with me.

I've been asked a few times how I felt as I was driving there, but I really could not describe it if I tried. I just knew that a conversation between my father and I had to happen that day. I knew that I had carried the shame, fear, guilt, hurt and baggage for long enough. And that every other time I had "forgiven" my father, was not the real deal because it wasn't about me letting go. I always wanted something from him: I wanted him to have missed me, to apologize, to admit what he did (which he still hasn't). I wanted him to say that he had thought about me all this time, that he had nightmares about what he did; that he felt bad. But this time was different: This time was all about me. This time was to free myself, and I had never felt so powerful in my life. To know that all the power that I had given him - not that he had taken from me – was now mine. On that day, I decided to no longer be a victim.

> *I remember arriving at my aunt's house, putting my car in park and thanking God for the power and courage to forgive him. I stepped out of my car, walked up the few stairs that lead to her front door and knocked; I was so calm. My aunt opened the door, and we walked through her house. A few of my cousins were sitting in the front room watching television and talking, so I waved, said hello and kept walking towards the back of the house in the direction of the kitchen where I found my father sitting at the kitchen table drinking a beer. I said hello and made small talk with my aunt. Before I knew it, I had boldly asked my father, "Can I talk to you for a minute outside?" He said yes, and followed me back through the house, out the front door. It still baffles me that he responded so calmly and casual, almost as if we always had a relationship, or as if him seeing me wasn't a surprise.*

Since that day when I told my mother about the things my father did to me, I had only seen him a few times. One of those times was when I was a freshman or sophomore in college, and was asked by the YMCA in Evansville to share how one of at risk teen programs (DIAMONDS) had affected my life.

> *After giving my presentation, I felt so powerful! I was a success story: I was the girl that had beaten the odds and didn't fall victim to the statistics of teen pregnancy, or being a high school dropout. I was on cloud nine and then I saw him; he must have been working there at the time. I was walking towards the restroom and stopped dead in my tracks.*
>
> *I felt like my feet were frozen to the floor, and I did not have control over my own body. I felt as if I had seen a ghost and whatever power I felt after presenting was gone. I had reverted back to that little girl, being held in my mother's arms. All the fear, shame and pain came flooding back. He called my name, and I took off running full speed. I ran into the restroom and prayed that he had not followed me, but I stood with my body pressed against the door just in case he had.*
>
> *I attempted to catch my breath, but all I could do was pray and cry. I prayed for God to help me breathe, because I could not. I prayed that my father would not try to enter the bathroom. I prayed that I could forget that everything ever happened, and that the abuse didn't affect me this way, but I knew better. After about 30 minutes, I was able to breathe again, so I washed my face, squared my shoulders and put my "strong black woman" mask*

on. I left the restroom, quickly walked back to my table, and ate dinner like nothing had happened.

On the front steps of my aunt's home, I remember telling my father "This will not take long, I just have a few things I want to say. I don't need you to say anything back. You don't need to admit anything, and you don't have to apologize to me for anything. I FORGIVE YOU. I forgive you for what you did, for the relationship we had and the relationship that we did not have."

In that moment, I felt free because I had released myself from being the victim. On that day, I decided to forgive him for what he did to me, and I also chose to forgive myself for all the decisions I made in the past where I allowed myself to blame him for my mistakes. From that day forward, I decided that my actions would be my own, my decisions would be my own, and I chose not to live in my victim mindset any longer. On that day, TRUE FORGIVENESS happened and my life has been forever changed. I, and the millions of women that have experienced sexual abuse are testaments that with true forgiveness, we can live and be happy. We can have healthy relationship, we can be loved, and we can give love. With true forgiveness, we can move past our pain, see beyond ourselves and help others. With true forgiveness, we are freed from the shackles of our past and can embark on a new journey towards the life we deserve, with an open heart and a freed soul.

End of chapter reflections

Chapter 3: Think about it
- What supports do you currently have to help you through tough moments in your life?
- What are you looking for in a therapist; what is your goal for seeing one?

Chapter 3: Take action
- Research different therapists to find one that is a good fit for you.
- Consistently visit with your therapist. Communicate openly and honestly with your therapist.
- Find established groups that support you and provided resources.

TAMESHA

Tamesha Allen is an inspirational speaker, author, youth advocate, educator, entrepreneur, and seminar leader. Allen helps others clarify values and passions, achieve a sense of balance, deepen their alliance with God, and grow through life transitions. Allen is the Founder and CEO of The Tallent Agency, LLC., where youth and young adults learn to embrace their gifts and talents. She is the leader of Forever Changed Prayer Ministry where the mission is, "Transforming God's people to live better lives."

Chapter 4

Faith vs. Fear

On June 27, 2011, I started my day just like any other day: I prayed, ate breakfast, and left for work. On my way to work, I listened to some gospel music on the radio station of AM 1310. I worked for a for-profit higher education institution in the registrar's department and, upon arrival, I had no idea that this particular day would be one of the best days of my life.

Once I arrived, I immediately clocked in and was asked to report to a conference room for a meeting. Not knowing what the meeting was about, I was a little nervous. As I entered the room, I saw around twenty to twenty-five other employees from different departments as well. At that point, I had a feeling that something was wrong. Shortly after, the director of the college came in and gave us her speech about the direction of the college and how she appreciated our service. She talked about how the college was downsizing and restructuring departments. In my mind, I said, "Yes! Today is the day!" The director talked for about thirty minutes, and honestly, I became bored after ten of those minutes.

At the end of her speech, she kindly thanked us again for our years of service and then told us that we were being laid off. As I looked around, I could tell that some of my co-workers were deeply saddened by this decision. My initial thought was, "Who lets people go on a Monday? Why not on a Friday? Why make people commute twenty to thirty minutes *just* to be let go?" I was more concerned about my gas tank than anything else. Once the director told us we were being laid-off she then mentioned how the process worked. *There is a process to being laid-off? How hard could it be to give someone a pink slip?* Obviously, I have never been laid-off before so this was all new to me. She explained that we will need to sign legal documentation, and we will also receive a severance check. Thereafter, she thanked us again, told us we had a few minutes to clean our desks, say our good-byes, and leave the premises.

I was not worried at all. In fact, I hurried to pack my belongings and say good-bye to all the co-workers I had developed a friendship with. However, there was on person who was not at their desk at the time of my departure; I was looking for my boss. I searched and searched, but could not find him anywhere. I just wanted to thank him for believing in me enough to help spread my wings and fly. He was one of the main people who believed that I had the skills to accomplish bigger and better things. I only had a few minutes though, so I could not continue to search for him.

After I said all my good-byes, I walked out those doors with a smile on my face. Once I arrived home that afternoon at 12:30 pm, reality begin to settle in. At that very moment, I realized I was unemployed. I had nowhere to report to for 10:00am on Tuesday morning. All types of questions ran through my mind. Questions like, "What am I going to do now?" "How will I support myself?" "Will I be able to find a job within the next few weeks?" "How will I tell my sister I lost my job?" I was terrified. One part of me wanted to call my former boss and ask if they would reconsider my termination and allow me to return to work the next day. However, the other part of me just said *forget it.* I did not know what to do, or how things would work out so I decided to call my mom to deliver the disturbing news.

> *phone rings*
> "Hey mom!" I said.
> "Hey Tamesha, what's going on?" She replied.
> "Well, I lost my job today."
> "Oh No! Well, it's going to be okay. The Lord will work everything out."

Now, in the back of my mind I thought, "Ummm…what??" I felt as though she only said that because she is my mom and needed to speak comforting words to me. Little did she know, I did not believe that God would work everything out at that moment in time. I was hurt, confused, lost, angry and still in disbelief. I was stuck!

While sitting at home, I reflected on what went wrong and why this had to happen to me. I could not understand it and I played the victim for the remainder of the day. A friend of mine called later and I told him what happened. He advised me to pray and ask God for His wisdom, knowledge and understanding. Now, I am a woman of great faith. I believe in God and have a relationship with Him. However, with the way I felt that day, I had nothing to say to God. I was too busy trying to figure out what my next move was going to be. Then I told myself, "Tamesha, pull yourself together girl. You are stronger than you think." So I did just that.

I sat down and began planning out what I needed to do in order to pass this spiritual test with flying colors. I knew I had a severance check coming in the mail soon, and I even thought about emptying out my 401K account, though doing that came with a penalty. All I knew was that this was about survival. I was not sure how long my unemployment situation would last (one month, three months, or six months); I just knew I had to get through it.

Later that evening, I was still pondering on how I was going to deliver the news to my sister. She was living with me while going to school - pursuing her Bachelor's degree in Social Work - so I knew the living situation may have needed to change for the both of us. Delivering bad news was not my expertise and, to make matters worse, she had recently bought a 42-inch plasma flat screen television as an appreciation gift for me. My heart dropped. I did not know what to say, or how to say it. I just knew that the more I prolonged telling her, the more difficult it would be.

> "Sis, I have something to tell you." I said.

"What?" She responded.
"I lost my job today."
"You did? Why?"
"I don't know."
"Well, this just means God has something better for you."

My sister's encouraging words blessed my soul. Although, I was still struggling with my faith, and God was still the farthest thing from my mind, I still needed for everything to be okay, but it was not. What was I supposed to do now? How was I going to support me and my sister? Yes, I had a little money in the bank, but it was not enough to last for a lengthy unemployment.

I informed my sister that once the lease was up, we would have to move into our own places because I could no longer support her. I felt terrible because I felt as though it was my fault that she had to fly on her own so soon. Later that night, I went into my bedroom and begin to lash out at God. "Why did you let this happen?" "I thought you loved me?" "What went wrong?" "What did I do to you to deserve this?" "I return a faithful tithe, active in the church and the community. Why Lord, Why me?" With tears flowing down my face, I was still trying to put the pieces of this puzzle together, but I came up with nothing. I felt like God had punished me for something I did that I knew nothing about and I did not know what to do. Somehow, I tried to keep the faith, and listen to the encouragement around me.

All throughout the night, several people called, texted and emailed me inspiring messages like, "You got this sis!", "The devil won't get the victory" and "The battle is not yours, it's the Lord's." One text came through that said, "Tamesha, you will get through this. You are not the only person who has lost a job." In a sense, I thought this was the rudest, most insensitive and most disrespectful statement ever said to me. I mean, who says, "You are not the only one....?" As I wiped my tears, I realized that my friend was right: I was not the only one who has lost a job. People lose their jobs left and right every day, but I was the victim, right? Wrong! Earlier that day, there were twenty-five other victims who had to figure out what their next move was going to be. How were they going to support their families? Will their current income suffice for a while? This feeling was all too common for several people. How do you cope when tragedy strikes? Do you quit? Do you tell God and forget it?

After about an hour of wrestling with God, I was an emotional wreck. I had cried so much I began to get a headache. My eyes were bloodshot red and puffed up to the point that I could not open them. Once I got up from my knees, I placed a lukewarm face towel on my eyes and laid down hoping my eyes would return to normal. While lying down, I was still pondering over my situation; this time, with a clearer head.

Although, I was shaken up spiritually, I knew something greater was about to take place; I just did not know when or where. Sometimes, God has to take us through in order for us to get to! "To what though?" was the million-dollar question. Was it repentance? Revival? Restoration? What in the world was God trying to show me? Then, this scripture came to mind, "...he will not let you be tempted beyond what you can bear..." 1st Cor. 10:13 (NIV). Really? God knew I could not bear this test. I had too much responsibility to go through this by myself and then it dawned on me: if God did not think you could not bear it, he would not have given it to you. Is this a joke? If so, this is not funny.

That night, I went to bed feeling fearful and alone. The next day, I woke with a new attitude and I felt optimistic about my situation. I could not allow the loss of my job to get the best of me. Yes, I was still shaken up about the whole thing, but everything happens for a reason. My sister reminded me to file for unemployment at the Indiana WorkOne office and, as I walked in and saw so many people, I did not realize how many families were impacted due companies reorganizing, or economic downfall. As I looked around, I saw some people I knew and some people I did not know. *WOW* was all I could say. I walked up to the information desk to receive a ticket from the receptionist and my number to be seen was seven, the current number that was being served was four. I thought that was too long of a wait and I was ready to get this part of my day over with. This place was crowded with people young and old; everyone was looking for employment and filing for their benefits. There was so much going on that I was tempted to leave, but then I thought about my livelihood so I waited, and waited, and waited some more. "Number seven!" *Yes!* I was next. As I approached the desk to be seen, I was so nervous.

> "How may I help you?" asked the customer service representative with smile on her face.
> "I am here to file for unemployment" I responded.
> "Have you ever filed before?"

"No, I have not." I replied, while fighting back tears. She then explained the process of how weekly unemployment benefits work. Once she was finished explaining, I had this distraught look on my face because I was completely shocked from all the items on the "to do list" in order to keep the benefits active: classes, workshops, seminars, and counseling. There was everything from resume writing to mock interviews, not to mention the job log that must be reported weekly. Calling, visiting and applying online trying to see if employers are hiring was a job itself and I was so emotionally drained, I could not keep up. The craziest thing was that my benefits would not start until after I received my severance check according to the customer service representative. Once I received that, it may *still* take another four to six weeks until my benefits started. *Whoa..whoa..whoa…what? Did I hear her correctly?* I could not believe this. I kindly explained to her that my livelihood was at risk and that there was absolutely no way I would be able to wait that long for my first benefits check. Then, he told me how much I would be receiving and tears began to flow down my face right in front of her.

I walked away from her desk feeling defeated. My income was literally cut in half: I went from making $33,134 a year to $15,536 with unemployment. This happened within all a years' time. The year 2011 to 2012 was rough and I was already budgeting. My budget was now tighter and I needed to adjust quickly. My feelings were hurt and life as I knew it was becoming progressively worse; I did not know how to overcome this test God had given me.

There is an old saying, "when life throws you lemons, make lemonade." Well, that all sounds great, but how was I supposed to make lemonade if I could not afford the pitcher? I had to figure out something. Not really knowing what that something was, I had to call on the one person I knew I could count on: my cousin who is currently serving in the United States Navy and although we are cousins, we were raised like brother and sister. As a matter of fact, there are four of us total: my sister, him, his brother and I all grew up together because our mothers wanted us to be close. Needless to say, if we needed anything my cousin was always there for us.

A few days went by and I was trying to figure out how to explain to my cousin that I had lost my job and needed a little financial help. I was already embarrassed to inform my other friends and family that were close to me and now I have to tell him too? I was in disbelief. My monthly expenses was about $1000 a month, which was almost one paycheck! Tithe, offering, rent, utilities, car payment, phone bill and food were all part of my needs; I really did not have time for too many wants because when I was not working, I was involved at church, or doing community service.

During this time, my severance check arrived and was able to cover my bills for that July. There was now a little breathing room, but not much. I felt as though the walls were closing in on me because when it came time for August's bills, things were not looking any better. Again, I had to figure out a way to ask my cousin for some help, but I was so fearful because I did not want to bother him with my burdens, and he had his own family to support. I finally got the courage to put my pride, fear and negative thoughts aside and called him. The phone rang, and I did not know what to expect.

"Hey cuz what's up?" He answered.
"Hey cuz! How are you? What are you doing? I miss you!" I responded nervously.
"I'm good, what's going on with you?"
"Well, I do not know how to tell you this, but I am going to say it anyway."
"Are you ok? What do you need to tell me? Is the family good?"
"All is well!"
"Then, what's wrong Mesha?"

With tears rolling down my face, I said. "I lost my job a few days ago, and I have very little money to pay for my bills next month. I have filed for unemployment, but that will not start until maybe four to six weeks." Without any hesitation he said, "How much do you need?" I replied, "Whatever you can send would be great." He said, "Ok, I will send you some money." We both said *I love you*, and hung up the phone. I did not ask for a specific dollar amount because I was already embarrassed to call and ask him for help.

A few days later, I received a check for $800.00 and I was so ecstatic and thankful that my cousin was willing to help. *But how did he know how much I needed? Did God reveal it to him? Or maybe he just wanted to send that much just in case I needed a little more.* I was not sure how he knew, but I was grateful. That money was enough to pay my bills for the month and not long after my cousin sent the check, I also received my unemployment debit card in the mail as well. *Yes!* I was so relieved, but my heart was still a little weary because my income was cut in half.

I activated my card and, that following week, I started receiving my benefits: $347 a week was what I was receiving to maintain my household. Things were tight. I started to find more ways to save and cut back on my expenses. If it was not on sale, or if I could not use a coupon, then I did not purchase it; I did not have enough to splurge, and had to make do with what I had. There were times of struggle: I experienced disconnection and eviction notices. I could not even afford to put gas in my car and I almost robbed God. Yes, you read correctly. I barely had enough to return my tithe and offering, but somehow, God always made a way when there was no way to be made.

My heart was troubled and I questioned if God would really come through for me. I felt as though I was fighting this battle by myself and keeping my head above water was no longer an option; it was a requirement. In the end, all I could think about was staying positive in knowing things would turnaround for my good.

Takeaways:

1. No matter what, your struggle does not override your strength. With every test, there is a testimony.
2. Never accept what the devil throws at you. Your life is worth more than what you realize.

Exercise:

Write two or three struggles you are currently enduring right now. What is your plan of action to recover?

Chapter 5

Just Believe

As the weeks passed, I finally began to wrap my mind around my unemployment situation; in order for me to come to terms with what happened, I had to keep my emotions under control and not allow myself to get further off track than I already was. You never know what to expect or how to react when *life happens.* You just have to learn how to deal with the issue at hand.

While I was attending all the different unemployment classes and applying for jobs, I took the opportunity to devote more time into a local non-profit organization. This organization helped to restore hope in the lives of homeless women and children, and have partnered with four homeless shelters to provide employment workshops, back-to-school rallies, celebrating Christmas, and much more.

Two of the shelters housed domestic violent victims, another housed women who paid their debt to society and were ready to start over, and the last shelter provided emergency housing for families. As my involvement with this organization grew stronger, it showed me how blessed I really was because you never know what someone else is going through. These women and children suffered several scars on every level. For some, they did not know how they would bounce back, because it felt like they were at a dead end. For others, they knew things would get better and that their destiny was on the way.

I loved visiting these shelters, and made it a part of my ministry to inspire, uplift, pray, and educate them on how bright their future was. The founder and president of the organization had a passion for these women to strive for better daily. She created a non-judgmental atmosphere that was full of love and support. She wanted these women to be encouraged in spite of their circumstances.

One day, after leaving an event from one of the shelters, I went home and cried. I was so emotional, and did not know why at first; I just knew things were not as bad as I made them to be, so I went into my room and prayed. It was the type of prayer you pray when you need clarity and a breakthrough all at the same time; I just began to talk to God and said, "Lord, I need you right now to give me peace that passes all understanding. Show me the way that I may be pleasing to your eyes Father God. I know I am undeserving of your grace and mercy. I just ask you give me the strength to endure this test right now. Bless me with your wisdom so that I can become better every day, in Jesus' name, Amen."

It was not a long and drawn out prayer, but short, sweet and straight to the point. I had to come to terms with the fact that God's will is the best way for my life! There was no other way. I had been turning to everyone else, when God was there the whole time, waiting on me to surrender my all. In the beginning, I was not sure how to surrender my heart to God completely. As I mentioned before, I am a woman of faith and I have a relationship with God, but I still struggle at times. Why, you may ask? I am human. I see how others endure tests and trials and wonder how they make it through. At this point, I knew I had no other choice but to persevere. I finally realized that I spent more time complaining and feeling sorry for myself, when I should have been giving thanks to God more than ever before. By ministering to the women at the shelters, it helped me understand that God is still in control. My problems were like small potatoes compared to anyone else's.

I had a reality check! I was not homeless, and I had food and clothes on my back; I even had a car to drive in. I may not have had all the things I *wanted*, but I did I have all the things I *needed* because God provided them for me. I felt like my faith was being restored; I would talk to God and He would talk back. I found myself spending more time with God daily and, though I had some good and bad days, in the end, I did my absolute best not to complain. I woke up every day with a smile on my face. Every time I walked into the unemployment office, I felt great about the jobs I applied for. Even if I was denied, I knew one day there would be an offer on the way.

The classes I attended were informative and insightful; our instructor made sure we were prepared to re-enter the workforce. Skills such as policy, resume development, interview question and answering had changed over the years, so he wanted us to be up to date. He encouraged us to take all opportunities to find employment seriously. While going through this process, I found out that the test was all about progress. You see, I knew there was something to learn for my unemployment expertise, though at the time, I had no clue to what it was. I did believe God wanted my undivided attention so I had to rethink how I was handling this test; I could not only pass, but I could also be a testimony to others.

The closer I drew to God, the nearer God drew to me. During this time, I felt more comfortable trusting God. I had to learn to leave things in God's hands and let Him work it out on my behalf. Oftentimes, we as humans believe we can handle things on our own. We become arrogant in our thinking and try to do what only God can, and yet still, we fail; we tend to make things a lot worse than what they were before. There are lessons in life, and we must learn and grow from them. Have you ever heard the phrase, "trials and tribulations come to make you stronger?" Even though this is a cliché that Christians often use, it's true! I did not believe in this common principle; I always felt people only said it because it sounded good. Another one I here all the time is, "this too shall pass", but what exactly does that mean? Should I rejoice, or be concerned after my current situation passes. Will my emotions be different from before? Nevertheless, I knew God had all the answers to any problem that needed solving.

One night, while getting ready for bed, I was preparing my heart and mind for prayer. Before I talk to God, I take a few moments of quiet time to clear my mind so that I am not distracted by the phone, television, etc. This prayer was different from all my previous prayers: right before I said *Amen*, God said, "Daughter, I have listened to you, now it's time for you to listen to me." Immediately, I stopped and listened to what God had to say. God said, "I need for you to trust me more." That's it? Well, He was right. I desired to trust God more, but did not know how. We all have dealt with, or maybe still are dealing, with trusting people. Trust is something that is earned, not given and I am big on trust. If I cannot trust you, then let's just say I know where to place you in my life. I needed for God to show me how to trust Him. No matter what it took, I wanted to be closer to Him. There were times I thought God had forgotten about me, but he hadn't; my problem was that I was operating in the flesh and not in the Holy Spirit.

One day, in our unemployment class, the instructor asked us to share our stories. I am a private person and do not like to disclose my personal business to anyone, but I knew this would help me and maybe someone else in their own struggle. One man shared that he was laid off his job after being there for twenty years; he was almost ready for retirement. Another lady was laid off because her company filed for bankruptcy; she was there for fifteen years earning a six figured salary. Can you imagine being devoted to a company, earning that type of income yearly, only to be decreased to a little over $300.00 a week? We all had stories. The beautiful thing about sharing your story is that, it helps people understand that better days are ahead. Each week, I would file for my benefits, apply for jobs, and attend classes. Then, I realized that routine was getting old.

One morning, I decided to step out on faith and call a local high school to inquire about speaking to their students. I have always desired to become a public speaker, but did not know what type of speaker I wanted to be at the time. I spoke to the assistant principal and he agreed to allow me to come and speak to the kids about believing in themselves.

The youth and young adults have always been close to my heart because I know life is not easy to bear, so when the day came for me to speak, I was so excited! I walked into a lecture hall of about fifteen young ladies; this was my opportunity to have what I call, girl talk. The ninety-minute session was based on peer pressure, dating, and self-identity. The young ladies opened up about the daily challenges they were facing. I would just allow them to talk while I listened. In the end, I provided some concrete advice for the ladies to consider, and it was awesome because they received me so well. They were attentive to what I had to say and appreciated me for coming. From that day forward, I knew what my God-given purpose was: public speaking.

We all have a gift that will make room for us. "A gift opens the way and ushers the giver into the presence of the great." Prov. 18:16. (NIV). There is nothing like waking up every morning doing what you love to do. Would you do what you love, even if it meant that you would not be compensated for it? I did. From January 2012 to June 2012, I spoke at various events for free. Not because I had to, but because I wanted to; building my network, sharpening my skills, and broadening my experience was my number one goal at the time. I was not concerned about money because no one really knew who I was. At times though, I did receive small tokens of appreciation such as gas cards, gift cards, dinners, etc. It was these little things that mattered to me the most.

For about a year and a half, I booked speaking engagements consistently. Then, one day, a friend of mine advised me to become a professional speaker. I was not really sure how this would happen; I just knew that if I work hard and stay dedicated, then things will pay off in the end. All throughout my life, people have complimented me on my speaking. They would often share feedback on how eloquent my speaking was, but for a while, I did not see what they saw; not necessarily because I did not believe in myself, but because I was just humbled and thankful that people saw something special about me. I decided to take my speaking a step further and used my skills to pray. Wherever the Lord needed me, I was there. As time passed, another speaking opportunity came my way for me to teach a face-to-face course at a higher education institution where I alum.

One day, I went to visit one of my mentors who worked as a Liberal Arts advisor. I was with her for a while, then, in the midst of my visit, I asked her if the institution was hiring. I explained to her that I was diligently seeking an employment opportunity to teach in a face-to-face setting. I shared with her my background in higher education and how I love educating young adults. She advised me to send my resume to the program chair who was over the Foundation of Success department, and I did just that. Within a few days, I received a phone call from the program chair to schedule an interview. When the day of my interviewed arrived, I immediately prayed and asked God to lead me. I said, "Lord, You know what I need. You know the desires of my heart. Let Your will be done." I walked into the interview with confidence knowing that I would walk out with the teaching position.

The program chair greeted me with a smile and a handshake.
"Hello Tamesha!" she said.
"Hello!" I replied. "How is your day going?"
"It's going well."
"Great! So tell me a little bit about yourself."
"Well, I have been in higher education for a quite some time now. I love working with youth and young adults. My passion speaks for itself. I hope to one day own my own business in connecting youth and young adults to their purpose in life. I believe in higher education. Students are my top priority."
"Great! It sounds like you are well experienced, and love what you do."
"Yes, I do!"
"Well, this teaching position requires a lot of patience, tough love, and sacrifice. The Foundation of Success strives to help students transition from one phase to the next on their academic journey. We teach life skills students can use in and outside the classroom such as; getting on course, accepting personal responsibility, self-motivation, time management, employing interdependence, gaining self-awareness, critical thinking, and emotional intelligence. Do you think this is a class you are interesting in teaching?"
"Yes...Yes...Yes!" I shouted
"Great! I will call you in a few days to work out the details. Welcome aboard! She said."
"Thank you so much!"

I was filled with excitement because teaching this course was going to help me grow on so many levels. I was blessed and ready to start right away.

On August 20, 2012, I started my first day of teaching twenty-five students. I was so nervous because I did not know how the students would receive me, but I did my best to not let it show; the only thing I knew, was that I was ready to work. I walked into a classroom full of scholars aged from eighteen to seventy five years old. Needless to say, that first day was more of an introduction day. I allowed the class to introduce themselves one by one, and I introduced myself last. It was so amazing to listen to the students share their names, programs of study, and occupations. We all took time to get to know each other and network together. I am strong believer in networking, and I emphasize how important it is for students to adopt a networking attitude daily.

After the introductions, I split the room into sections to play a game called, "Do you remember me?" One by one, each student had to exchange information about themselves to each other at their tables. Once everyone was finished, the first person who shared had to try to recite what each of their peers said. The first team to get each person's information correctly won a small prize. This game went on for an hour, but the students really enjoyed getting to know one another. Not only did it help their memory, it also encouraged them to build their network.

After the game, I decided to dive a little deeper with my class on some of the challenges they faced as students. One student mentioned stereotypes. Well, of course, we all experience various stereotypes. However, this particular student mentioned how people view her differently based on her race and religion. These two areas are some of the most common topics of discussion when it comes to stereotypes. I decided to tread lightly and reassure my students that all opinions count so that no one would become offended. The student shared that she is a proud African American woman who loves God, and she went on to explain that there is a big difference between religion and relationship. This student was raised in the Baptist church so her beliefs were no jewelry, no pants, no make-up, etc. She then mentioned that one day, she was walking on campus from one building to another when someone stopped her and asked if she was Apostolic because she was wearing a skirt. She proceeded to tell them *no*, and went on her way.

She then asked this question: "Ms. Allen, why do people assume you are one way based on who you are or what you look like?" As I listened to her question, I had no clue how I was going to respond so I thought about what she said previously, and responded with, "You are beautiful, and no one can take that away from you. It is unfortunate that we live in a society where people make assumptions based off of what they think and not what they actually know." She said, "I totally agree with you. Thank you Ms. Allen."

Yes! I felt like an MVT (Most Valuable Teacher) in that moment. As class went on, the dialogue got a little deeper. Students begin to ask bold questions about sexual identity, illnesses, fashion and food, and I shared with my students my thoughts on humanity as a whole. We as a people differ in many ways; nobody is the same. I then posed the question, "What if everyone in the world were the same? How would we relate to one another? Would we become bored?" I continued, "God created us to be different because we are special in His eyes. There is great purpose for all of our lives, and that should never be taken for granted. Don't allow haters distract you from what you were created to do; be the best you that you can be!" Their facial expressions lit up like a light bulb and it reminded me of why I love working in higher education:

it's not just about teaching the students, but also about learning from them. God blessed me with that teaching position so that I can be a light into people's lives. I was so ready to start that new chapter and I thank God for restoration.

Takeaways:

1. God will never put no more on you than you can bear.
2. You may be down but never out. He will take care of every need no matter what.

Exercise:

Close your eyes. Think about previous situations where God has brought you through the storm. How did you feel? What was your reaction?

Chapter 6

My Comeback

After my class, I felt good about myself. I knew that God's divine purpose for my life was important; I just did not know how important. I was aiming to make a positive impact on my students, and nailed it. Honestly, I expected becoming an educator to be more challenging than I experienced. As a matter of fact, I allowed fear to settle in and I did not believe that this profession would suit me. All I knew was that I desired to be a professional public speaker. This profession requires skills such as confidence, creativity, high energy, exceptional vocabulary, and more. Although I believed these qualifications fit me well, I still struggled with a little doubt. Higher education is one of the most rewarding professions to work in: the face-to-face contact with students is wonderful, not to mention the professional network with faculty and staff is great as well.

I learned years ago, one main key to success is network...network...network! Everybody needs somebody to help them grow to the next level in life, so I had already established working relationships with individuals prior to my employment. We all should desire increase, whether it is spiritually, physically, professionally, or financially; everyone should learn to strive for the better. Needless to say, the opportunity of me becoming an educator was a part of my purpose. I strongly believe God prepared me for the moment to help shape the lives of students daily, and I give my 100 percent to all my students. You never know who God will place in your pathway to encourage and speak life into. I cherish every moment I have, and make sure all students I encounter with succeed.

Throughout the semester, I ask my student these questions: Why are you here? How bad do you want success? What are you willing to sacrifice in order to succeed? Usually, students respond like, "I want it really bad Ms. Allen", or "I am here because of want a better life for my family", or "I am the first generation to attend college", or "...because I want to be financially stable". When I hear responses such as these, my heart is overjoyed because I know I am living my dream. One quality I have is determination: I live, eat, breath, and sleep this word because it defines who I am. This word has helped shape me to be the loving, personable, bold, and strong woman I am today.

One day, I shared with my students that life is full of choices, whether good or bad; they have the power to choose their own direction. If someone chooses to go left when he or she should have gone right, then that person would reap those consequences. However, if choosing to stay stagnant, then life will eventually pass you by. Once I finished talking, they all had astounded looks on their faces. My overall goal is not just to educate, but also to motivate and to be an inspiration to my students. The experiences with my students made me realize that my purpose is to help other people find what God has chosen them to be.

In addition to being an educator, I had another project I was working on for the youth and young adults: I was blessed with an opportunity to present a workshop called, "What is my talent?" to a youth group at a local church and they loved it! Yes…Yes…Yes! After the workshop, I went home and thanked God for His wonderful works and for using me to empower the youth. A few days later, I received a phone call requesting that I speak to some young adult women for a women's day program. I accepted, and spoke on one of my popular topics: Beauty is Your Name. Those ladies were in tears before, after, and during the event; not because they felt emotionally burdened, but because they felt revived, restored, and renewed. It was then that I knew it was time for me to take my profession to a higher level and become an entrepreneur. I always knew the day would come when I would be my own boss, I just did not know when.

After those speaking engagements, I decided to take the time to do some soul searching. I needed God's direction on what my next step was going to be. You see, God is not the author of confusion and neither am I. I fell to my knees and prayed, "Lord please order my steps. You know me, and the desires of my heart; all I want to do is please you. In Jesus' name, Amen." Once I finished praying, I was directed to this passage of scripture: "Being confident of this, that he who began a good work in you will carry it onto completion until the day of Christ Jesus." Phil. 1:6 NIV. I read this text over and over again, and it helped me to understand my purpose completely.

Becoming an entrepreneur was risky; I did not know the first thing to do, or how to establish a business. As the day went on, I remembered that I knew a woman who could assist me with branding my business. She is an expert in helping aspiring entrepreneurs to launch their businesses. So I called her, and we agreed to meet at a coffee shop the next day. When we met, she shared with me how proud and excited she was of me for launching my own business. She explained the ins and outs of how to brand a business through a detailed, yet complex model; that was my interpretation at least. Even with my undergraduate degree in business administration, I did not realize how tedious this process was and I was a little intimated by the layout she presented. However, I was familiar with some of the elements outlined in the model: Name of Business, Mission, Vision, and Core Values.

As we continued, she had other key principles listed such as *list your "why?", list at least five to seven strategic action steps for your business, list at least three to five reasons why people should do business with you, name two things that makes you different,* and the list went on and on. At first, I felt so overwhelmed, and I just wanted to say, "forget this! I do not want to start a business anymore!" Though the conversation continued, I just did not know how to respond.

> Then she asked, "Tamesha, will you be selling products too?"
> I said, "yes, eventually."
> "Have you thought about a name for your brand?"
> "Yes, it will be called, Purpose of Power."
> "Ok", she said hesitantly. "What does that mean? Who is your target audience?"

"The name represents people embracing their purpose by understanding how powerful it is, and my target audience is youth and young adults from ages thirteen to twenty-five."

"Ok, let's come back to the name and the target audience later. Have you thought about a logo?"

"Yes, I would like to have a purple rose. Purple, because it's my favorite color and a rose because it's my favorite flower."

"Why a rose? What does that symbolize?"

"I have no idea; I just like it because it's my favorite."

We paused, looked at each other and began laughing. "Tamesha, you have given me a lot to ponder. I truly have my work cut out for me, but I am looking forward to helping you start your entrepreneurial journey. Give me a few days, to tweak the name and logo. I will design something I know you will love and be proud of" She said.

"Ok, thank you so much. I'm super excited!"

In the beginning, I did not share with too many people that I was starting my own business, only because I knew everyone was not cheering for me to succeed. I am a discreet individual so what I choose to disclose, I make public and what I choose to be discreet about, I keep private. For weeks I had made the decision to be low key about the process and projects that I was working on, and focused on becoming a legal entity. After all I have been through these past couple of years, now was the time for me to walk into a new season of prosperity, power, and position. I just needed to make sure God was pleased with my efforts. I knew I had a lot to offer to people who were in need, especially youth and young adults, but I also knew that it was not my responsibility to save the world; Jesus Christ already had that mission covered. I just wanted to impact the world in such a way that people would believe again. *Believe in what?* you may ask: themselves.

People young and old need to know that someone is waiting to hear their testimony, their story, and their sacrifices on how they overcame their challenges in life.

Youth and young adults are near and dear to my heart. Most are facing unbearable issues everyday such as; peer pressure, sexual identity, self-identity, and abuse on every level. Young people are always searching for a way out so I wanted to provide a service that would help them refocus on what God has called them to do. I needed for them to know that their lives are important. It's my mission!

A few days went by, and my brand designer called me and asked me to pass by her house to see the design she created. As I pulled up to her house, I had no idea what to expect; I had mixed emotions at first. I walked into her house and she directed me to sit at the dining room table. I sat and was very nervous. She opened her laptop, showed me the design, and I almost cried. I was shocked and excited all at the same time. It was beautiful. She said, "Tamesha, I had to go to work on this one. I used your name and just added a cross at the end." My brand is called, *Tallent*, with two L's. I loved it because it was different, and the way she designed my logo stood out so people would know who I am. I thanked her over and over again for her creativity, love, support, and patience. It was almost like she read my mind and knew exactly what I was aiming for. After my visit, I went home, fell to my knees and thanked God for sending me someone who was an expert in branding businesses.

If I went to someone else, I probably would have not received the same love and support that I got from her; she had my best interest at heart, and I appreciated that. I was smiling ear to ear because I was so ecstatic about my new logo and walking into my new season.

A few more days passed, and I was ready to file the paperwork that legalized my business. I needed to be legal because I wanted people to know that this is not a side hustle. I was ready to build my clientele and the vision for my business was much bigger than a side gig; I am legit! I was so proud of myself because my status was changing to CEO and Founder of a registered business called *The Tallent Agency, LLC*. This was surreal to me; my mind could not fathom what was happening. I had become an official entrepreneur!

For thirty days, I prayed specifically for my business and its daily operation. I needed some reassurance in my decision and did not want disappoint God, or me. Every day, I declared - and still declare - victory and prosperity over my life, home, profession, students, and yes, my business as well. I never thought the day would come where I would see prosperity manifest itself ever so sweetly like the day I became my own boss. I came a long way, and still have a long way to go, but I am just so thankful for the process and progress that is being made. Running a business is not an easy task and it can be scarier than what people think. There is an old adage that says, "More money, more power, brings more responsibility." Another one says, "New levels, new devils", meaning that there is a price that comes with being the key decision maker: challenges will arise and you have to be "on your p's and q's" to address each one as an entrepreneur. I was not worried though; I was up for the challenge. Yes, I had good days and bad ones too, but I did my best not to complain.

There was a lot of prayer and preparation for this season of my life. I went from losing my job in June 2011, to starting over in August 2012, and launched a business in January 2014. When I look back over this timeline and how I made it though, I have no other choice but to give God all the praise, honor, and glory for what he has done in my life. There were days when I did not believe in myself. I felt I was not knowledgeable enough to be a leader, and I battled fear for days, weeks, and months at a time all because I did not believe. I almost allowed certain people to redirect my focus on something that God did not have for me, because there were days I did not think my dreams would become a reality. There were moments I wanted to throw in the towel and just give up everything I worked so hard for. There were times I spent hours crying over my finances, faith, and the so called *favor* I had with God. I asked questions like, "When will the pain end? When will it be my turn to succeed? How long do I have to endure such misery?" Little did I know, God was preparing me that whole time. Honestly, if God gave us the step by step blueprint to our lives, we probably would run in the other direction.

Everyone's journey is different. Sometimes, we look at everyone else and desire what they have. The reality is that you do not know what they went through in order for them to enjoy what you see that they have. In other words, you see their glory, but do not know their story. We all have a story to share, and it is supposed to show someone else how to escape their current situation. You see, life is not going to be all roses and butterflies, and some people believe that their life is not worth living. Well, I've stopped by to say, *Yes, it is! Victory is near.*

At one point, I did not know if I would ever become victorious over my trials and tribulations. I questioned God, not just because of my struggle, but because I had a difficult time believing. Sometimes, I felt lost and alone because I did not know who to turn to, or if I should turn to anyone. My life was turned upside down and I felt like a failure for a long time. Hitting rock bottom though, was not an option for me. I had goals and dreams of doing something awesome with my life. I did not plan for my journey to go the way it was; I had desired for life to be picture perfect. But this time was my time! I was ready to walk in the victory.

I learned that being victorious is more than just experiencing the finer things in life though. Anyone can obtain a nice car, large home, and have millions of dollars in the bank. Anyone can get married, have children, and travel the world at their leisure. So, what's my point? Well, you can have all these things, but what do you *really* have to show for your life? How many people have you encouraged? How many people's needs have you met? Whose life have you changed, even in the past day or two? When you rise in the morning, do you feel like your purpose has been fulfilled from the day before? All of these are questions that I had to think about. Not because of self-satisfaction, or a receiving a pat on the back, but because my heart desires to make a difference, so I strive for better daily. If I can impact one person's life, if I can inspire somebody to improve who they are, then I have done what God has called me to do. There is nothing wrong with having the desire to live a comfortable life. I just had to quickly learn that this was not true victory. True victory is being able to bring comfort to other people's lives, teaching them that their life matters just like anyone else's. When I realized this principle, then I understood I *am* victorious.

When I look at the people I love and inspire daily, that is my true victory. I wake up ready to give my 100 percent because that is what God chose me to do. There is nothing better than putting a smile on someone's face, or giving someone a hug, or providing a meal or two for someone. Victory is in knowing that the battle has already been won: no worrying, no fear, and no doubt. It's allowing things to happen the way they are supposed to, and when they are supposed to. Yes, I will still have challenges, we all do; but God is able and has kept me like never before. He has blessed me with so much more and I am living in the overflow of blessings because of His grace and mercy. I do not desire to have someone else's life. God created me to step up and standout amongst others; even if I have to stand alone, I will still stand. My faith has made me stronger. My experience has made me wiser. My heart has made me believe. I walk in the victory, not because of who I am but because of who God created me to be.

Takeaways:

1. Do what you love and do not hold back.
2. Write the vision and make it plain.

Exercise:

The bible says in Romans 12:3 "…God hath dealt to every man the measure of faith." What does this mean to you? How do you plan to grow your faith daily?

LEXI

Lexi Jones is an entrepreneur, transformational speaker, business & financial coach, strategist, and change agent, delivering mind shifting talks and workshops that disrupt the status quo resulting in transformational experiences. As an independent contractor for the nation's #1 financial marketing firm, Primerica Financial Services, she locates, trains, and develops leaders to build and run their own Primerica Offices. Lexi shares the practical and simple financial concepts that took her from bankrupt to legacy builder. Learn what banks and other traditional financial institutions will never teach you. Her motto is: "You are only confined by the walls you build for yourself." – Andrew Murphy. "With God all things are possible" – Matthew 19:26.

Chapter 7

Upleveling Your Money Mindset

In 2008, I lost everything: I lost my job, I lost my car, I lost my home and eventually, I lost my marriage. The downward financial spiral began in 2007 when my ex-husband lost his job. This was devastating to him as a man, but we were still able to make ends meet with my income. Though my ex-husband had a hard time with his unemployment, I did not worry: I was able to take care of things and knew that it would be a matter of time before he was employed again. However, we did not anticipate that I would lose my job months later. When I lost my job, we had very little savings because we used most of it when I was on maternity leave in 2006. The savings we had left only lasted about 3 months and I was out of work for 10 months. We were already having marital problems and the lack of money just magnified it all.

Ours was a horribly unhappy home. The children wouldn't come out of their rooms because all we did was argue. Eventually, we decided to file for bankruptcy. We were able to keep our home and car, but that only lasted for a few months until we lost those too. Things between my ex-husband and I had become even worse. Despite filing for bankruptcy, we were in debt again. I made the decision that we should separate and we were supposed to separate for a time and work on things, but we never could quite work it out. So, we ended up filing for divorce a couple of years later and the divorce was final another year or so after.

Here I was…single with three children, no permanent job, no home, no marriage and no plan. I felt embarrassed. I was in my early thirties and I felt like I disappointed my immediate and extended family. I felt that I had let down so many people who looked up to me. I felt like a failure. Then, depression set in. Now, unlike most people's perception of a depressed person (one who might stay indoors and stay in bed), I still showed up to meetings and other obligations; I still went to church and I attended friends' birthday parties, weddings, etc. I put on the greatest front ever, but inside, I was a ball of nothingness; I was broken, just going through the motions of life, not really living. To others, it didn't look like much had changed, but I knew I was not myself; I knew I was not performing at my usual level. You had to really know me in order to catch the real subtle difference in my behavior. Like a functional drunk, I was able to operate even in the midst of my depression. There were a couple of days here and there though, where I would shut down both mentally and physically. Most people just assumed that I was getting the rest I needed because I stayed very busy. But, I knew that if something did not change, I was going to explode.

Finally, I managed to secure a job and an apartment, but by this time, I was saddled with debt: I was stuck with all the debt from the marriage because most things had been in my name. My daily mail consisted of bills that had gone to collections and notices from the court stating that I was being sued for one debt or the other. The majority of my phone calls were from my good old buddies at the collection companies. They began calling me by my first name as if they were people I knew on a personal level. When I stopped answering my phone, they began calling my job. We had Caller ID at my job so I did not answer the calls there either. Then, it got really embarrassing: they began calling family, friends, and people I hadn't talked to in several years. They were relentless, I was hopeless, and I was running out of lies to tell family and friends. My world had fallen apart. Something had to give…Something had to change…I just wanted to be me again.

One night, everything hit me like a ton of bricks. I cried; I was doing a lot of this lately, but this time it was different. I cried and could not stop. I lay prostrate on my carpeted floor, crying out to God that I could not take anymore. I yelled out, "This could not possibly be my life forever!" I felt like I was being punished for the financial crap I was in, but mostly for divorcing my ex-husband. I felt like an incompetent parent. I could not go another day pretending everything was okay because it was not okay; I was dying inside and nobody knew. I had secured a great paying job, was promoted twice within a couple years, yet I still could not get ahead financially. I was tired…I was done. I wanted God to do something and to do it now; I felt God had been silent for far too long. When I got up from the floor the next morning however, I had no idea that God was going to answer my prayer in the way that he did; that day in March, 2011 changed my life forever.

The next morning, I peeled my face away from the carpet, got up, washed my face got the children up and we went through our usual morning routine. I took them to school and then I went to work. I put on the usual front, but was secretly waiting for the day to end so that I could pick up my children and go home. I was still asking God, *what was I missing? Why can't I get ahead financially?* I was begging God; *please do not let this be my life! What do I need to do?*

That afternoon, I needed to take some paperwork to the opposite end of my office building; I hardly ever had to go to that side because the building is very large and spread like a college campus. When I got there, I ran into a co-worker that I did not see very often because we were now in two different departments. She greeted me, and then out of the blue asked me if I wanted to sit down with her financial coach who was helping her with her finances. I responded, "Yes" and I thought to myself, *I was just praying for some kind of relief!* So she coordinated an appointment for her financial coach to meet me there at our job within the next couple days.

I was terribly excited and that morning I arose with a new hope. I could not wait for the meeting with this financial coach; I was more than ready to get my mess sorted out. There would be no shame in my game and I would tell him the bitter truth of it all. When lunch time arrived, I made my way to the designated meeting room where I, along with my co-worker, waited for the financial coach to arrive. When he arrived, he introduced himself to me and began his presentation. The more he shared with me, the more relieved and excited I became. He taught me a couple of financial concepts that were so simple I began to see light at the end of the tunnel. He only gave me a peek that day though; that was the objective of the appointment. I then needed to decide whether or not I wanted to continue with his services. In my mind's eye, this was a no brainer so we set another date and time to meet. This time, we would meet at my home and I would have all of the financial documents he requested. I was more than ready to get on the path to financial freedom.

When the financial coach came to my home, he taught me a few simple concepts that would forever change the way I thought about money and how I handled money. All of the stress and all of the frustration just went away after our 45-minute meeting. My debt was still there, but with what I learned and now understood about finances, I became mentally free. Finances and money management are about mindset; that was the very first thing I learned. In fact, it was the most important thing I learned that day. I learned that I was able to get out of debt, I learned how to save and I was able to get on the path to financial freedom. I had shifted my mindset. I no longer was a slave to money; money was now a tool that I had full control over. I was determined more than ever to apply all that he taught me. In 45 minutes, he had managed to change my world: five years of sheer hell overturned in 45 minutes!

I began putting these concepts to practice and I saw my debt disappearing, my savings growing and I became confident in my knowledge of money management. I was so excited about this change in my life that I asked my financial coach what I needed to do to help others the way he had helped me. I watched him, I learned and I did exactly as he instructed me to do. I got the appropriate licenses and there was no turning back. If you would have told me in 2007, that I would be teaching others how to get out of debt and maximize their savings, I would have laughed you into the sunset. I never liked math; heck, I never liked numbers! Anything that required me to do any kind of math, even simple math, I despised. But today, I can't imagine a life without sharing with and teaching others about the financial concepts that set me free. Helping others learn these concepts and watching them get free is one of the most rewarding experiences (and yes, I still hate math!). Well, by now, now you are probably wondering, what are these concepts?

In the following chapters, you are going to discover the simple and practical financial concepts I used - and continue to use - on my path to financial freedom. I am going to share with you three keys to financial independence and, when followed, many have become debt free and have maximized their savings. The first key is that you must up level your money mindset. From my story above, it may seem that I had a shift in my money mindset as soon as I had those couple of meetings with my financial coach, when in actuality, it took me years to get to that point. Not only did it take me years to achieve, but it also took devastation and loss before I was ready for change. I was at the point where I was so hurt that I *needed* the change. I then learned enough to *want* the change and finally, I understood that time was of the essence and I *had* to change.

If you are reading this, but are not at a point of desperation, my advice to you is to read and implement the concepts presented here to avoid potential money pitfalls. If you are reading this book and you are at the point of desperation, you're hurting and you want a change, take a huge sigh of relief; I have your answer. By the time you are finished reading about these three keys, you will be ready to implement change in a way that lasts a lifetime.

So how do you up level your money mindset? How long does it take? The length of time is solely dependent upon you; you are in total control. Changing the mindset is simply a re-training of the brain. The beliefs and values we have around money are beliefs and values that were taught to us in childhood. In order to up level your money mindset, you must first confront the negative money messages and beliefs that you may have. If you look at any problem area in your life, you will find limiting beliefs at the root. Limiting beliefs are imbedded deeply in our subconscious mind; we may not even be aware that they are the source of our actions and they are hurdles to our success. They stop us from reaching our full potential and this is the case even in finance.

Our habits can be traced back to limiting beliefs and poor attitudes towards money. They are the foundation of our financial behavior because though our childhood is over, we may still carry them with us, embedded from our parents' discussions and behaviors. Some examples of negative money messages are:

- Money is the root of all evil
- Those who are rich are greedy
- Money is a tool used for power and control
- Money is an end, not a means to an end
- High debt is normal
- Everyone goes to their grave with debt
- Only those with a whole lot of money can financially independent

Have you heard of any of these negative money messages? Were any of these taught to you? Can you think of a couple more negative money messages? Write them down here:

_____
_____
_____
_____
_____
_____
_____
_____

Now that you have identified some more negative money messages, can you determine where they came from? Were they statements explicitly stated by family or other influential adults? What behaviors did they exhibit that reinforced those messages? Write your discoveries here:

_____
_____
_____
_____
_____
_____
_____
_____

After you have identified and confronted your negative money messages, the next step is to rewrite them; you must turn them into positive money messages. An important way to rewrite negative money messages is to turn them into affirmations: affirmations are goals expressed as if they are already achieved. Once you rewrite them, you must repeat them daily and you might even repeat them two to three times a day. Here are a couple of positive money messages (money affirmations):

- Money is a resource for health and wealth.
- Money can be used to create my own rewards.
- I feel good about money and deserve it in my life.
- Great wealth is flowing to me now.
- Money flows to me easily.
- I choose wealth and abundance.
- Whatever I do, it always ends in amassing wealth in my life.
- I clearly see opportunities to effortlessly make money.

How does repeating affirmations actually work? Affirmations, when done correctly, retrain the mind. It is not necessary for you to believe them at first, but what is necessary is repeating them throughout the day. We naturally train ourselves to concentrate on what we do not have so we must train our mind to focus on abundance so that we can experience abundance. What we focus on, we will experience more of. How can you make positive money messages/affirmations to your daily routine?

_____
_____
_____
_____
_____

In addition to re-training your brain using positive money messages/affirmations, developing a money philosophy is essential to up leveling your money mindset because your money philosophy is your view on money. When you have a money philosophy, you can then align your money behaviors with it. An example of a negative money philosophy is, "Money is a path to happiness". If this is your philosophy, you are likely to experience a lot of frustration. You are literally giving money the power and control whether you are happy or not. An example of a positive money philosophy is, "Give more, save more, live more" by Peter Anderson. My money philosophy is, "Leave a legacy for generations to come". Can you see how these positive money philosophies promote healthy money management? The following are some questions you can ponder to help develop your own positive money philosophy:

- What are my long-term financial goals? Why are they important to me?
- Which financial goals am I now meeting? Which ones are not being met?
- What specific behaviors must I adopt in order to meet all my financial goals?
- What are the benefits of my current spending habits? What are the disadvantages?
- What do I like about giving? What do I dislike?

- What am I most likely to buy on impulse?
- What makes a purchase worthwhile?
- What makes a purchase wasteful?
- What is my definition of overspending?
- How do I differentiate luxury and necessity?
- What did I learn about money growing up that I now think is true?
- What did I learn about money growing up that I now think is false?
- What rationalizations do I use to justify overspending?
- What has to happen to me in order for me to stick to my budget?

Ponder these questions and determine your money philosophy. What did you come up with? Write it here:

_____
_____
_____
_____

Up leveling your money mindset is the first key number because without it you will not be able to take action on the next two keys; this is mandatory. Your negative money messages must be confronted, rewritten and repeated daily in order to re-train the brain. Our thoughts become our actions and if you do not have a healthy perspective on money, you cannot expect to have a healthy relationship with money. If you do not have a healthy relationship with money, you cannot expect to be successful in money management. If you are not successful in money management, you cannot get out of debt, maximize savings and get on the path to financial freedom. Your path to money success begins when you are ready to confront the mindset that keeps you defeated.

Are you willing to do what it takes to up level your money mindset? If so, you are ready to discover the next key: how to build a stable financial home. There is an order to building your financial home. Many of us begin building our financial home with everything but the foundation. When building a physical home, it is imperative that the contractor/builder begins with the foundation. If the foundation is not right, the whole house will eventually come down. The same applies when building your financial home. If you do not begin with the foundation, the house will eventually come down.

Chapter 8

Building Your Financial Home

I Timothy 5:8 says, "If anyone does not provide for his relatives, and especially for his immediate family, he has denied the faith and is worse than an unbeliever." Even if you are a family of one, you are responsible for financially providing for your family. When it comes to building your financial home, there is a proper way to do so. If you are like me and the average person in our society, we are not educated on how money really works. I remember learning how to write a check in high school, but that was the extent of learning how to manage money. My parents did their best to teach us what they knew: pay your tithe, pay your bills, and save what you can. Unbeknownst to my parents, their behavior and conversations about money were conditioning us to live under a lack mindset.

Just like building a literal home, laying the foundation to your financial home is essential. If the foundation is not laid properly, the entire house will come falling down. The foundation of establishing your financial home is mindset. Mindset is everything. But before we delve into this, here is how the financial home should be built:

- Mindset
- Income Protection
- Emergency Fund
- Debt Elimination
- Retirement
- Other Goals and Dreams

Often times, we begin with other goals and dreams. We take vacations and spend a lot of money on leisure. In and of itself, there is nothing wrong with that. However, if you are spending a lot of money on this without having the rest of your financial home in order, then that is problematic.

Mindset

If we look at any problem area in our lives, we will find limiting beliefs at the root. Limiting beliefs are embedded so deeply in our subconscious mind that we aren't even aware that they are the source of our thoughts and actions. They are hurdles to our success and they stop us from reaching our full potential. This is the case even in our finances. Our habits can be traced back to limiting beliefs and poor attitudes towards money. They are the foundation of our financial behavior, often developed in childhood. Though our childhood is over, we carry with us things that we have concluded from our parent's discussions and behaviors. If the mindset is not addressed – no matter how much you know about properly building your financial home - you will not be able to build your financial home and sustain it for the long haul. Because of that, much of this chapter will be spent on mindset. Mindset can be tough to change, but it is possible. Two major ways is by adopting positive money messages and developing your money philosophy.

Money Messages

Before you can adopt positive money messages, you must first become aware of, and confront your negative money messages. As mentioned before, many negative money messages are introduced during our childhood. They may have been explicitly stated or derived from various money related instances and events. Here are some examples of money messages.

- Money is the root of all evil.
- Those who are rich are greedy.
- Money is a tool used for power and control.
- Money is an end, not a means to an end.
- Live for today. No need to save. The future does not matter.
- I am not smart enough or capable enough to make a lot of money.
- High debt is normal.
- The more money you make, the happier you will be.
- In a relationship, the man makes all of the financial decisions.
- I am not supposed to talk about money.
- I must work long hours and neglect family in order to earn good income.
- Buying expensive gifts proves that I love someone.
- I will never have enough.
- The government or social security will take care of me later in life.

Do any of these negative money messages resonate with you? We know that money messages can be introduced in our childhood, but where exactly do they come from? Parents, other caring adults, institutions of education, and institutions of religion are just some of the places where they may originate. For example, you may have often observed our parents fighting about money and stressing about bills, or perhaps your parents did not discuss money at all; maybe they made a big deal of, or complained about having to spend money. Church leaders and members may have also shared the view that "true" or "righteous" Christians are poor.

What negative money messages did you grow up with?

_____
_____
_____
_____
_____
_____

During your childhood, what behaviors did you witness that may have reinforced the negative money messages you identified?

_____
_____
_____
_____
_____
_____

Once negative money messages have been identified and confronted, they must be rewritten into positive money messages. One way to do this is to turn them into affirmations. Affirmations are goals expressed as if they have already been achieved. They are repeated daily and even several times per day. Here are a couple of positive money messages (affirmations).

- Money is a resource for health and wealth.
- Money can be used to create my own rewards.
- I feel good about money and deserve it in my life.
- Great wealth is flowing to me now.
- Money flows to me easily.
- I choose wealth and abundance.
- Whatever I do, it always ends in amassing wealth in my life.
- I clearly see opportunities to effortlessly make money.

How do affirmations work? Do they really work? To affirm something means to declare that it is true and, when done correctly, affirmations retrain the mind. It is not necessary that you believe them at first. What is necessary, is repeating them throughout the day, every day. Typically, we train ourselves to concentrate on what we do not have. What I believe is what we focus on, is what we will experience more of. We must train our mind to focus on abundance so that we can experience more abundance.

What are your thoughts about affirmations? How will you apply positive money messages/affirmations as a part of your daily routine?

_____

_____

_____

_____

_____

_____

Your Money Philosophy

Identifying your money philosophy is essential. It provides your view on money which affects how you manage your money. It also provides your purpose to manage your money. Think of it like a mission statement: what is your overall mission and purpose on this earth? How will you align your money goals and habits with your personal mission? If you view money as the only path to happiness, you are likely to experience a lot of frustration, and this kind of philosophy will land you in a lot of debt. Below are some questions that will help you think about the purpose for your money management habits and develop your money philosophy.

- What are my long-term financial goals?
- Why are these goals important to me?
- Which financial goals am I now meeting? Which ones are not being met?
- What specific behaviors must I adopt in order to meet all my financial goals?
- What are the benefits to my current spending habits? What are the drawbacks?
- What do I like about gift giving? What do I dislike?
- What am I most likely to buy on impulse?
- What makes a purchase worthwhile?
- What makes a purchase wasteful?
- What is my definition of overspending?
- How do I differentiate luxury and necessity?
- What did I learn about money growing up that I now think is true?
- What did I learn about money growing up that I now think is false?
- What rationalizations do I use to justify overspending?
- What would have to happen for me to stick to my budget?

My personal money philosophy is: Leave a legacy for generations to come
By legacy, I don't just mean a legacy of money; I also mean a legacy of education. Because of this money philosophy, educating myself and others is a priority and my spending habits follow. Another financial guru, Peter Anderson, states that his money philosophy is – Give more. Save more. Live more.

After working through the above questions and reviewing the examples provided, what have you determined your money philosophy to be?

_____
_____
_____
_____
_____
_____

Once your mindset is where it needs to be, you will be better equipped to properly build your financial home. It is also highly likely that you'd sustain this properly built home for the long-term. Now, let's build the rest of the house.

Income Protection

One of the first tangible steps to financial freedom an individual or family must take is to protect their income, and you can do so by purchasing life insurance. Several people have their reasons why they don't purchase life insurance and the most common are:
- It costs too much
- I don't know anything about it
- It really isn't that important.

Let me ask you this: If you had a car, a house, and a tree, which would you insure? When I ask the people who attend my workshops or presentations, most would say the house, some say they would insure the car, but both groups of people agree that the tree would definitely not be an option. Now, let me ask you this: If the tree grew money on it weekly or bi-weekly, which would you insure now? I bet your answer is the tree! Your answer would be the same as everyone else's. What if I told you that this tree is you? If you bring home income weekly, bi-weekly, or monthly and something happened to you, the loss of income would be devastating to your family. For those of you who are single, I know you may be thinking that you have no need for income protection because you do not have a spouse and/or children depending on you. However, life insurance is important, and it does not have to cost an arm and a leg if you can get educated on the right kind of insurance to purchase, even if you're single.

Why life insurance is important

I have seen many families, in my time, who have been financially affected by the loss of a loved one. Families have had to find different ways to raise money to bury their loved one and may have lost homes, or become overwhelmed with debt as a result. This is not the kind of "providing for your family" that the Bible speaks about. Many families cannot grieve the way they want and need to because of the sudden financial stress of death. Be responsible. Your family does not deserve this. Your life insurance coverage can take care of burial expenses, outstanding debt, and income replacement and, if you have small children, you may even want to include money for their education. If you have any children with disabilities, you may want to include some money to help with that as well.

For those of you who are single, you still have a responsibility to your family. We never know the day or the hour when we will draw our last breath. Just because you aren't married and don't have any children, does not mean that someone will not be financially affected by your death. Somebody has to pay for your funeral (or cremation) when you die, so at minimum, burial expenses should be provided for. If you have debt, then your coverage should include any outstanding debt as well; it is the responsible thing to do. You might be asking; how do I know how much coverage I need? To determine this, use the acronym DIME:

Debt $_____
Income Replacement $_____
(How many years of income do you want to provide for your family? This is usually based on age of your children)
Mortgage $_____
Expenses (funeral) $_____

The cost of the right kind of life insurance

If you have the right kind of life insurance, it will not cost you that much. There are two types of life insurance: whole life or cash value, and term life. Whole life insurance (cash value) comes with a savings attached to it. Term life is strictly your death benefit. If there is one thing you should remember from this section is, **never bundle your life insurance and savings**. Many insurance companies sell whole life insurance at high prices simply because it is more lucrative for them; they operate similarly to banks in that a portion of your premium goes towards your savings (investment), but the insurance company will make large returns off of your money and only give you 3 – 4%. It does not matter what kind of whole life insurance you have (variable life, universal life, etc.), you are only going to get 3-4%. Later in this chapter, when I talk about investing, you will see why 3-4% is highway robbery. Agents selling whole life, like to tout the savings as an awesome reason to purchase whole life: they will tell you that you can borrow from it to pay for your children's education, or to put a down payment on your home, or for whatever you may need.

What they do not clearly explain to you is that you must pay that back at 6-8% interest. You should be asking, "If I am only earning 3-4%, why do I have to pay it back at 6-8%? Why do I have to pay it back? Isn't it my money?" Oh, and by the way, you don't begin collecting anything in that savings until you have had it for 3 – 4 years. If this isn't enough of a rip off, when you die, your family will only get the death benefit, or the savings; they will not get both. Yes, you read correctly. Even though their premiums covered the death benefit and the savings, your family will only get one or the other, not both.

Term life insurance is strictly a death benefit; there are no savings attached to it. You should, or rather must, do your savings/investments on your own, separate from life insurance. In the event you die, your family will receive the life insurance and the investments. A largely accepted misconception is that we are supposed to have life insurance for the rest of our lives. This couldn't be further from the truth. The purpose of life insurance is to create an immediate estate in times where you do not have enough savings. However, at some point if we have been saving/investing like we should, we get to a point where we can self-sustain, and have no need for any type of life insurance.

Finally, level term is the type of term insurance you want because your premiums would never change throughout the term of the insurance. Term insurance is sold in 5-year, 10-year, 15 -ear, 20-year, 25-year, 30-year, and 35-year terms. You choose the term based on the number of years it would take you to become self-sustaining. We will talk more about this when we discuss savings/investing.

Emergency Fund

According to CNBC (June, 2016), 66 million Americans do not have an emergency fund. CNBC further reported that Generation X fared the worst when it came to being prepared for a sudden expenses. According to the Wall Street Journal, one in four Americans have no emergency savings. In a time when expenses seem to grow faster than most have the ability to save, many are discouraged and feel saving is something that is nearly impossible.

While expenses are getting more expensive at a faster rate, everyone can save. First, you have to understand that it is not about what you earn; it is about what you keep. There are people who are successfully saving even though they make $10/hour or less. What are they doing you ask? Two things:

1. They have made a commitment to the pay themselves first at all costs. This advice isn't something new; many of us have heard this. I heard it often growing up as my mother taught us the envelope system: the first two envelopes we always put money in was tithe/offering and savings. Somewhere along the road, I picked up from parents that bills had to be paid at all costs. Pay the bills, pay the bills, and pay the bills. As I became an adult, instead of being committed to paying myself first, I became committed to paying the bills first. If you think you understand me to say pay yourself before paying bills, you are correct. If you think you understand me say that the bills can wait, you are correct. Here is what I know. When you haven an emergency, or even when you retire, your utility company, your cell phone company, your credit card company, or any other creditor will be sending you a check to help you out. Now, I am not advocating all out irresponsibility with your bills, but what I am saying is to live within your means; do not create unnecessary expenses, and above all, pay yourself first. Your emergency savings should be used for just that; true emergencies. It should not be used to pay the light bill when your income check will come soon and can take care of it then. Instead, call the utility company and make an arrangement for payment.

2. They minimize, if not eliminate, wasteful spending. No matter the income, every client I have ever worked with has indulged in wasteful spending. The area with the most waste is eating out. I have seen individuals and families spend hundreds of dollars a month on places like Starbucks, McDonalds, Burger King, Wendys, Olive Garden, snacks from the gas station and more.

Not only is having an emergency fund important, but where you save, even generally, is critically important. Since you are not using your emergency fund every day, it should be in an account where it will have significant growth. It should also be in a place where you can have access but in the traditional sense. Your contributions should be automatic and we will talk more about this in the next chapter. As we segue into savings/investing, here is an exercise to help you put some things into perspective. Calculate how much you've earned and how much you've saved over your working lifetime.

A) Average annual income (estimate): _____
B) Times number of years worked: x_____
C) Equals total amount earned: = _____
D) Amount of your current personal savings: _____
E) Divide D by C: = _____%

This equals your percentage of income saved. How did you do?

Chapter 9

Saving & Investing – Building Your Financial Home Continued

The next part of building your financial home is saving and investing. In the last chapter, I mentioned that how you save is just as important as saving. In this context, saving is referring to investing. I do not believe in saving at or through a bank if you are looking to retire and stay retired, or if you are looking for financial freedom. I know you must be thinking, *that is a bold statement.* You are probably also thinking *why wouldn't you save at or through a bank? The bank is the safest place to save.* Permit me to share with you a concept that forever changed the way I look at saving. Before I learned of this, I too believed that the bank was the safest place to save, if I could save anything; I also believed that there was no way that I could save money living paycheck to paycheck, even after a couple of promotions. I just could not get ahead. Then, I learned about the Rule of 72.

The Rule of 72 is a concept that explains why the rich are rich and the poor are poor. It may seem like a very complex thing, but it is actually a very simple concept that anyone can understand. The Rule of 72 simply says that you take the number 72 and divide it by your rate of return. This tells you the number of years it will take for your money to double. This simple concept is a game changer! Let me give you an example: as you may or may not know, the rate of return on any savings account, at any bank or credit union, is anywhere between .01% and .04%. For easy math's sake, let's say your rate of return on your bank's savings account is 1%. You go to the bank with $100 and you tell the banker that you want to deposit your $100 into your savings. You also ask the banker when your $100 will become $200. Using the rule of 72, you would take 72 and divide it by 1 (rate of return). I will give you a moment to do the math…Pretend the *Jeopardy*! music is playing right now. Have you figured it out?

How many years is it going to take for your $100 to become $200? If you said 72 years, you are correct! That's right, you've done the math correctly; 72 years! Who has time to wait 72 years for $100 to become $200? I don't, and I'm guessing neither do you. If that took 72 years, imagine how many years it would take using the actual rate of return between .01 - .04%. Of course, this is a one-time deposit, but even if you deposit monthly, your money will not grow at the rate you need it to grow to meet your goal of financial freedom – retiring and staying retired. It would even take forever for you to realize any short term goals.

Saving at a bank is a guaranteed loss; you can say bye-bye to a lasting retirement because you will eventually have to return to work. Now that we understand this concept, it is recommended that everyone have 3 types of savings – emergency, short-term, and long term (wealth building, retirement). Where should you do any significant saving? One of the places where you should save is by investing in the market. *Isn't the market risky?* Yes. *Doesn't it cost a lot to invest?* No. *Isn't it too complicated to learn?* No. *What savings should I invest?* You should invest your emergency fund, your short term savings (money you will use in about 5 years), and your long-term savings (retirement, wealth building). *What? My emergency fund too?* Yes, even your emergency fund. Your emergency fund can be invested in municipal bonds. These investments are backed by the government so they have low risk and are the safest of most investments. They are also highly liquid which means that you can sell your shares quickly for cash whenever you have an emergency (it usually takes about 48 hours if you are doing the transaction online). Based on historical performance, these types of investments can return anywhere from 3-6%, and even up to 9%. This is surely better than the bank's .01 - .04%.

As for your short term investments, something like a Roth IRA would be ideal: you can withdraw with no penalty after 5 years in most cases and in some, less than 5 years. Your wealth building (retirement – think 401k, 403b, Traditional Roth) investment is something you do not touch until you are 59 ½ years old. Many people do not have any emergency savings or a short term savings, though some have a retirement account of some kind. When they run into financial hardship or need a significant amount of money for something they deem very important, they withdraw from their wealth building account. When this is done, there are stiff penalties. You pay taxes and a penalty for early withdrawal. After paying the fees, it was almost not worth withdrawing.

This is why it is important to have 2 – 3 types of savings. There are a couple things one should ask him/herself when saving, whether it is for something in the very short future, or for something long term. Ask yourself, "What is the objective of the savings (emergency, a short term goal like a house or car, or something long term like retirement)? What is my savings goal (the amount you would like the savings to reach)? "How long it will take to reach that goal?" These questions help you to decide what kind of savings you need.

I feel you thinking; you may be saying, *I have a short term savings or long term savings through your bank. What is wrong with that?* The issue with that the rate of return: the bank is the middle man, so you better believe that they are going to get their cut of your return. This is how banks, credit card companies and other traditional financial institutions stay in business. It is important that you invest with an investment company directly. You have more choices and control over your investments. You also cut out a middle man that is going to take a significant portion of your returns. Take a look at this chart that illustrates the importance of rate of return. The higher the rate of return, the better it is for you. But, the only way you will realize high returns, is to cut out the middle man.

Number of Years	3% Return	6% Return	12% Return
0	$10,000	$10,000	$10,000
6			$20,000
12		$20,000	$40,000
18			$80,000
24	$20,000	$40,000	$160,000
30			$320,000
36		$80,000	$640,000
42			$1,280,000
48	$40,000	$160,000	$2,560,000

Based on the Rule of 72, a one-time contribution of $10,000 doubles 4 more times at 12% than at 3%.

It is unlikely that an investment would grow 10% or more on a consistent basis.

Another thing to watch for are fees. Fees are one of the reasons why the 401k, 403b, and other similar investments do not perform well. If your return is 9% but your fees are 4.5%, you are only getting a 4.5% return. Many advertisements will state there is a 6% return, when in actuality there may only be a 3% return after fees. Below is a list of about 10 different fees that can impact the growth of your investments. While you do not need to memorize all of these types of fees, it is essential to know that they exist. Keep your fees low so that you can get to financial freedom quickly.

1. Transaction Costs – this is a broad category that can include brokerage commissions, spread costs, and market impact costs. This is can be the most expensive fee.
2. Purchase Fee – this is a charge that goes directly to the fund company.
3. Sales Charge (Load Charge) – This is a charge that is paid to the broker. There are three types of loads A (front load), B, and C (Back end). The best type of Sales charge is an A (front end load). You are charged upfront.
4. Redemption Fee – this is a fee for selling your shares
5. Tax Costs – this fee is actually charged for "administrative" fees. (particularly for those investments that are tax deferred like the 401k.)
6. Account fee – some funds charge a maintenance fee for the account
7. Soft Dollar Costs – these are costs that normally fund managers should pay. However, they are disguised and the investor ends up paying for trading costs.
8. Expense Ratio – this is the main fee that they will advertise. Just remember this does not include everything.
9. Exchange fee – this is a fee to move or exchange from one fund to another within the same family of funds.
10. Cash Drag – this is the amount of cash that fund managers keep on hand to satisfy any redemptions (selling of shares). It is not a direct fee but it does take away from performance.

Do you have a 401k? Here is a resource to when it comes to saving for your future, your methods for saving must be diverse. You know the old saying, "Don't put all of your eggs in one basket"? It applies here as well. Warren Buffet says, "Don't test the depth of a river with both feet." Investments are one way of improving your chances for successful savings (whether it's saving for an emergency, short-term, or long-term). If you have a 401k, you still should have an investment outside of your employer. One resource to check on how your 401k is performing is the website americasbest401k.com.

Other ways to add to your savings portfolio are real estate investing, investing in gold or silver, and oil and mineral rights. Though we can't address all of the possible investment avenues in this book, hopefully what we do cover will open your eyes to various ways to build your financially stable home as it relates to savings and investing. You never want to put all of your assets into one type of investment. Once again, I highly suggest you find a financial coach to guide you along the way. The remainder of this chapter will address this along with developing a plan and executing it.

Hiring a financial coach can be a daunting task. After all, who can you trust? How do you know if they are telling you the right thing? Will they look out for your well-being or only for the well-being of the company they work for? Is the expense of hiring a financial coach worth it? For this reason, some people never get to the point of developing an educated financial plan, and some people prefer to do it themselves. It is not impossible, but it takes a long time and one can also expect to make more mistakes this way. So what do you look for in a financial advisor? Look for an independent fiduciary rather than a broker. A broker is paid commissions to sell. They only offer products and services that must be approved by their employer, and their commissions are nondeductible. They themselves are the custodian of their funds. The only standard they have to meet is a suitability standard. This means they only have to make sure that the investment you participate in matches your investor profile. They aren't that much concerned with whether or not it performs the best for your needs.

An independent fiduciary – one that is registered by the state - however, is paid a flat fee or low commissions for their advice, and their advisory fees may be deductible. They are independent which means that they are not constrained or employed by the organization. All fees are transparent and the fiduciary does not receive compensation for trading stocks or bonds because they use a third-party custodian: meaning your funds do not stay with them. An example of third party custodians could be Primerica Financial Services, Fidelity, or Schwab. These firms have access to various products and services from investment companies, and they are legally bound to provide advice along with any disclosure of conflicts. Finally, an independent fiduciary has a fiduciary standard. This means that they are concerned first and foremost about your well-being and the well-being of your funds.

After finding a financial coach - a fiduciary - you want to have a financial needs analysis done. This is a fancy phrase for your financial plan. The Bible says, "My people perish for a lack of vision." It also says *write the vision and make it plain*, ant this goes for your financial planning as well. It is not enough to know the components of a financially stable home; you need a plan for achieving it. The financial needs analysis is like your financial GPS: it includes everything from income protection, auto/home insurance, debt elimination, to savings and investments. The one thing most people do not do, is look at the various financial aspects of their home in a holistic way. Your plan for getting out of debt impacts your income protection plan. Your income protection plan impacts your saving/investing plan and vice versa. Your savings/investing plan is impacted by your debt elimination plan... *You get the picture, right?* Once again, a financial needs analysis should not cost you an arm and a leg. There are fiduciaries that will do free financial needs analysis. My clients are always excited about getting the financial needs analysis because it is the road map to financial freedom.

I remember when I first had my financial needs analysis done. Upon receiving it, I felt relieved, excited, and optimistic about my financial future. I did not have to stress about how I was going to get back on track financially. I didn't have to stress about how I was going to get out of debt. I did not have to worry about my ability to save. I had the papers in my hand with a plan. Even though, I hadn't begun anything yet, I was able to sleep better that night because I had a step by step plan that would lead me to financial freedom; no more financial overwhelm. Once I had the plan in my hand that was not the end; I actually had to put the plan in place. Unfortunately, several people stop right here.

The actual execution of the plan is something altogether different. This is where we come full circle to what we learned in the first chapter of this section. Mindset is everything: if you do not have the proper mindset, your financial needs analysis will be just a stack of papers that will go in a drawer, or on a shelf, maybe never seeing the light of day again. Because of this, it is important to stay in close contact with your financial coach/fiduciary during the beginning of execution; they are there to hold you accountable. If you did a great job of re-writing your negative money messages into positive ones, developing your money philosophy, and establishing your financial goals, this will help you to stay focused, be disciplined, and execute successfully.

The plan must be reviewed periodically. It is not a set it and forget it type thing. I suggest a yearly review and also whenever there are life changes that impact the financial plan like job loss, change of jobs, increase in pay, decrease in pay, birth of a new child, adding a spouse, losing a spouse, etc. Believe it or not, anyone can get wealthy, and any decision you make, to protect your income, to start an emergency savings, to invest, to diversify is a start. Staying wealthy though, is another issue. How your financial assets are allocated will makes all the difference. This is another reason why having a financial coach/fiduciary is important. They can help you to determine if any changes are needed in your allocations. Asset allocation is your long term strategy for diversifying your investments whether in the stock market, real estate investing, oil and mineral rights, etc.

Once you have established your financial home...
1. Mindset
2. Income protection
3. Emergency Fund
4. Savings/Investing

...you are truly on your way to financial freedom. This is when you can do all of the things you enjoy doing without worrying if it may impact the essential aspects of your financial home. You can take that vacation without worrying about what financial struggles await you when you return. You don't have to worry about "robbing Peter to pay Paul". You don't have to worry about whether or not you can retire. You can sleep better at night. You can enjoy life.

Anyone can become wealthy once they have the right information to do so. Many of us have stood by for too long talking about which entities don't want us to become wealthy and financially independent, while banks, credit card companies and other traditional financial institutions do not want us to know the truth about financial freedom; the information is out there.

We must understand that we can get out of debt, we can save, and we can become financially free. It took me experiencing the loss of my job, my home, my car, and my husband, before I thought there *had* to be another way. Once I opened my mind to doing things differently, all the information I needed began to surface. I met my financial coach and took action. I did not make any more excuses. I did not cast any more blame. I recognized that I had total control over my financial future, and I didn't look back.

All that is left to do is to make the commitment to self: make the commitment to up-level your mindset and to properly build your financial home. My heartfelt desire is that you will allow the words in these three chapters to move you to take control of your life. Make the commitment to becoming financially free, changing your life and the lives of generations to come.

SCOTT

Scott Dawson is a native to Indianapolis, IN where he spent his years growing up and graduating from Pike high school. After high school he joined the United States Marine Corps and later went on to receive his bachelor's degree in business administration with a concentration in project management from Capella University. Scott has chosen to continue on with his education by working on achieving his masters and doctorate degrees. Scott has been an inspiration in the local communities and churches around the city of Indianapolis, IN. Scott uses his passion for photography to capture a person's beauty, and his knowledge, experience and voice to show people just how beautiful they really are. Scott's love for helping others has always been his biggest passion and purpose in life. Scott looks forward to motivating, inspiring, and helping the transformation of those who he comes in contact with, leaving them better than when they first came.

Chapter 10

Mindset

When most of us are looking to succeed in life, we look to others for answers, directions, or some other type of helpful tip. Most times, we never look in the mirror and realize that we already have all the answers to be successful. Success, simply put, is saying that you're going to do something and then doing it. Some of us have to learn this lesson the hard way and others may have to continually be taught the lesson, until understood. For me growing up for me wasn't the easiest but it wasn't the worst either.

My story can be summed up in one word: PAIN. I'm sure there are lots of others who can relate, or who may even have a different word to sum up their life's story. Mine is pain because, at a young age, someone that I trusted to protect me violated that trust and caused me great pain. In life, one thing that we're never taught in school is how to deal with our pain. Instead, we are spoken to, disciplined, or given detention and, for some extreme situations, we're recommended to a counselor for our issues.

The problem then becomes the fact that the issue we may now have was never our own, but was passed on to us by someone else who hadn't gotten their own issues resolved. At a young age I didn't know what to say, how to say what, or who to say it to. You think you can tell those you love and care about, but you're often left confused once it's a person you trust, love, and care about. Your mind starts to convince you that you are the problem and that's why something happened, or that the situation is normal because you don't know better. My father took that trust from me at an early age and left me to raise myself from that point on without a positive male role model.

I was left confused and unprotected so my first instinct was to look out for myself and put up a guard against all men. The fact that a man had caused me pain, and had also betrayed my trust, only left me to assume that all men were the same so I took to women at an early age to find peace and refuge. My father was rarely home so my mother had to provide for me and my brother all by herself; my mother was a strong woman and she did everything she could to keep a roof over our heads, food on the table and clothes on our backs.

I struggled in school because of everything that was happening to me. When the people that I loved and cared about left, I felt abandoned; people were constantly coming and going in and out of my life. There wasn't much stability growing up and, for a while, we went through a tough period of being homeless. There was never a place to call home and we were constantly moving from place to place so I quickly learned how to live without and not become attached to things. It wasn't hard to leave friends behind because I never really had many.

Where I lived growing up, everyone only cared about sports, but because of my size and weight, I wasn't the most athletic person. That didn't totally bother me even though I was always being humiliated by my brother in front of everyone; I would just stay indoors, away from the psychological tear down sessions he would put on me. I really didn't know what to do, or how to ignore him. I'm sure my brother was going through his own pain, and he seemed to use me as the point of release in order to take out his frustration. Even though most days my brother acted like he didn't know me, I still loved him and would do anything for him.

Growing up in the hood, there were plenty of cold nights and hot summer days. My mother would have to turn on the oven in the kitchen to try to warm the house, and boil hot water just so we could take a bath; this was our norm for the longest time. We shared the house with rats and roaches and would take turns giving one another a scare or two when we'd come across each other. Despite the rodents, we still kept a clean house because one, we weren't dirty people and, two, we had nothing to get dirty. These roaches and rodents would come from next door, upstairs, or from the walls and floors. These were some of the tough times I endured growing up while I was supposed to be focusing on my education.

I really hadn't known what I wanted to be growing up because no one I knew had done anything or had gone anywhere. I couldn't say I wanted to be a doctor or lawyer because I never knew or saw one other than on the Cosby show. It wasn't until my high school years that I finally learned what I wanted to do when I graduated. The only problem was that I was not on track for graduating. I had previously been held back, and that sore memory was painful, but not enough to want to be accepted more by my peers than graduate. When the time came to make that final decision of being liked by my peers or graduating; the first thing I was taught by a great mentor was that mindset is everything what you tell yourself is truth whether positive or negative. I had to make a life decision: did I want to remain in the same place, or should I move on?

I made the choice to move on. The way I had figured it, things couldn't get any worse than what they had been for me the past few years. I had to suck up my pride, buckle down and agree to retake a lot of underclassmen courses in order to graduate. I wanted to become a Marine, but couldn't join without a high school diploma. It's funny how when we want something bad enough, we know how to go after it until we achieve it. That's what mindset does: it allows you to focus on your goal and achieve it. Willpower comes from mindset.

Not only did I have to graduate high school, I also had to lose 90lbs from being heavily over weight by the Marine Corps weight standards. Again, everything would fall back on how badly I wanted to reach my goals. I learned that when you want something as bad as you want to breathe then you will be successful. The mind tells the body what it can and cannot do. If you want it bad enough, the mind will not even allow room in your mind for "can nots" to exist. You have to start where you are with, with what you have, for what you have is plenty. I remember hearing my mentor speak growing up with so much conviction; I didn't understand where he got that kind of energy for life.

I listened to his story and realized that his wasn't much different from mine; that gave me the hope I needed to see my way through and accomplish my goal. I had found my reason for the success I wanted so badly. I wanted to get away from the area I lived in and the people that I allowed to hold me back. I also knew that if I hadn't gotten away, it would be a miracle to see my 21st birthday alive or not end up in prison with the way things were going around town. I made it happen; it was a proud moment for me to have my mother watch me graduate from high school.

I wanted to prove to myself, and everyone else, that I wasn't a loser. I knew when I came back from recruit training that things would be different and I would be much stronger. The Marines broke me down and raised me up a stronger man. The friends that I once knew didn't seem interesting anymore because they were still doing the same things from high school. My mind was now more focused on the future and getting ahead. The military taught me a wealth of things that have transferred over into my personal life and helped give me more discipline in my thoughts and actions.

I remember the moment when I first really understood that God had a purpose for my life. My unit had been up going on almost 72 hours in a fire fight to take over this city that the insurgents were using as a strong hold; they were housing a lot of weapons that were killing a lot of the troops. We hadn't eaten, or slept a wink; we were also just about dehydrated because of the heat and lack of water. After about three days, we were finally able to secure the city and return to our base. In the process of taking off my gear and body armor after that long battle, I noticed a small hole where light was coming through.

It surprised me because I didn't recall getting shot throughout all the exchange of gun fire. When I looked at where the hole was located in my armor, I noticed that it was right over my chest pocket. I then checked my body for any injuries, but I didn't find any. I then remembered that I always had a mini-Bible in my chest pocket when I went out on missions. To my surprise, lodged inside of that bible was the bullet meant to take me out. It had penetrated the Bible but had not gone all the way through.

At that very moment, I dropped to the ground and wept like a baby because I knew that I was saved only by the grace of God. God had spared my life and I knew I did not deserve it. I knew because of certain things in my past and the things being done in combat, there could be no logical reason as to why God would, or should, spare my life. That day, I knew there was something more to me and God slowly started to reveal that to me. It wasn't until sometime after that incident that God revealed that His plan would require me to go back to school.

I laughed so hard because all I could think on was my earlier experience of repeating a grade and barely graduating high school. I, like Jonah from the Bible, decided to do my own thing; life is funny and God can be even funnier because He allows us to feel that we have some type of control over our life. He gives us the gift of choices but somehow, your life doesn't become peaceful and your nights don't stop being restless until you find out what that purpose is and why He chose you. At this point in my life, I had been making all the wrong decisions and getting in relationships with all the wrong people.

After falling on my butt and continuously going through hard times, I began to listen to God more. I finally enrolled in college and took a few classes; I felt that was good enough and let school go. That only made the journey harder and longer for me because I didn't see the reason for what I was supposed to be doing. I did just about everything I could and created excuses as to why I didn't have the time to do school. God then reminded me that He can read minds and also knows the future, and I realized I had lost yet another battle with God.

Then, one day, a good friend of mine was thinking about taking his life because his girlfriend was cheating on him with one of his close friends. Well, the Marine in me wanted to say, "let's pack our gear and handle this" but, for some reason, that feeling took a back seat and God started speaking to me on the seriousness of that situation. He helped give me the words to help save his life; there is where I really learned that the tongue has power and can speak life or death into anyone. I began to take school a lot more seriously after that, though I was not totally sure what path I was being directed to go.

Though I had gotten further into my schooling, graduation had still seemed a ways off; I could only put one foot forward. I learned so much through my failures because the professors were truly earning their paychecks with me in their class. I had come home for a while on vacation from overseas and attended a few church revivals and for some reason, I just felt God was calling me to be a minister. I laughed so hard at that thought, I gave myself a headache. I thought to myself that I couldn't give up the women and the pretty good life I was finally living now, but God said he had something else planned for me.

Little did I know, He wasn't trying to tell me to become a pastor; He was showing me that I have the gift of speaking to people. I learned that everything that God gives you to say has power and He created us with ears to be able to hear what is being spoken. At the end of my undergraduate journey, I looked back and realized it took me eight years to get a traditionally four-year degree and truly, I was the one who had created that time gap. My situation reminded me of the children of Israel from the Bible that it took them forty years to go somewhere that some scholars suggest was only a 3-day journey away.

I learned that when you're blind you'll tell yourself something is what it's not, and vice versa. The journey was tough but was powerful and enlightening into what God has in store for me. Going through that struggle with school was God's way of teaching me to first speak life into myself before being able to speak life into anyone else. When I crossed that stage it was as if an instant light bulb was triggered in my head and God spoke to me clear as day. He told me that everything that I went through was never about me; I had to go through it, to be able to speak on it, in order to help someone else. It's so funny to me how we can be so selfish and make so many things about ourselves. Because of that nature, we cause ourselves more problems than we ever needed to have by not listening to what God is telling us to do.

My walk was my walk for a reason and that was to help someone out of their season. God could have let me go several times, but He didn't and every day I spend my life being grateful that He didn't. I dedicate my life and time to Him now, helping others find their purpose in their passion.

Take Away:

1. Don't try to hide or bury your pain, draw from your pain to strengthen yourself.
2. Even if no one accepts you, you have to accept yourself.
3. Everything isn't about you.
4. Stop interrupting God and telling Him what you want and need, and listen to what He wants to give you.

Exercise:

1. Make it a point to wake up with a purpose to do something for someone else that day.
2. Write something great about yourself for each day of the month and on that day speak life into yourself.
3. Work on making sure your efforts match the life you are wanting to have.

Chapter 11

What is your "WHY"

It took for me to encounter certain situations in order to see the reasons behind them. The funny thing is that life gives you clues and shows you flags along the way. I had just been living my life for me, and I thought that was good enough because it was my life to do as I pleased. Growing up in church, it sometimes wasn't enough to do for others because I never saw what they were doing for me. God quickly had to show me my wrong and that took a lot of my early years to learn that lesson. After graduation, I learned more of my purpose but, still didn't understand why me and what for. Speaking was something that seemed to come naturally, but what did I have to say and for what reason?

At this time, I still hadn't learned my why for everything God was showing me. From just having gone through a horrible divorce, I had to learn to love myself and give back to others. I especially had to show more love to my daughter because in that marriage, she got neglected because my wife was jealous of her and our relationship. I quickly learned that since she's my only child, she looks up to me as her protector, provider, and role model. I had to think to myself, *was I living up to what she needed?* and realized, in that moment, that I hadn't been doing so. I quickly did a re-assessment on myself and my life and find out what needed to be worked on and I knew than that my daughter was my why.

My daughter just wasn't some child; she is my child. Even with going through a rough time having my father in and out of my life whenever he wanted, I vowed to not be that man; to be there to support her, and to show her what a man is supposed to be. Having a good job was not good enough for me to say that was enough. She motivated me to stay in school and to keep going until I obtain my PhD. It's funny how we rub off on kids because in our nightly prayers I hear her asking God to one day allow her to get her PhD. She asked for that on her own, and that was the first step towards confirmation that I'm walking in my why because now, I understand it better.

When you find your why and self-assess, you have to be completely honest with yourself. No one else matters at that point because transparency is key. For me, understanding that my daughter is my why it was not about what I thought or felt would be best for me but best for her and her future. When you find your why you don't have to wait for that alarm clock to go off because your why will give you that drive to get up on your own and grind. After graduating with my Bachelor's, I was fired from my job and not given any reason at all. That was so unexpected and I was not financially prepared for the hardships to come.

I was denied food stamps because I was in college, and I was given very little unemployment benefits since my last job's salary didn't pay much; most of what I did get, ended up going towards child support. At this, I could have given up because nothing was going well. But what would that have solved, or made better? Absolutely nothing. At the end of the day, I had a little girl who still needed to eat, have freshly washed clothes, and get to and from school; that wasn't going to happen on its own. Because she is my why, I had to realize that my situation doesn't define who I am. I had to realize how *bad do I want it*.

Many times, people get caught up in the hype of talking about all the things they want to do or are going to do and that sounds sexy to them and other people. The truth is that actions speak louder than words. After getting laid off, my daughter saw me get up and grind harder than she probably had ever seen. She knew I stayed up working on my school assignments, and would sometimes put a cover over me because I fell asleep in my chair, or on the couch. She saw the passion I had to give us a better life and not take for granted what we had. God is awesome because He provided all of our needs: I was never late on a bill, or any payments, and I still to this day don't know how I was getting it done, but I know it was due to God's grace and mercy.

I wanted so bad to be out of that situation that my why drove me every day to learn more and network with everyone that I came into contact with. I started putting together business plans and writing a book. By the time I finished writing my first book, I had a way to make some income. I started a nonprofit that provides scholarships so that others, who may have been in my place, won't have to wonder where their help is. It wasn't about me. Still, I was showing that in helping ourselves we must also help others. I told my daughter that she is my why and that I live every day for God and her, and that He will provide all our needs. I'm glad that she was able to see that.

Instead of complaining about what I wanted or needed, she instead saw me get up every day and go after it. She liked hearing me speak to adults and kids, and seeing the changes that were coming into their lives for the positive. Sometimes I'd hear her in her room playing, imitating me by speaking to her dolls or a class of students. She'd repeat my words and add some pretty powerful words of her own that I've often borrowed. It's funny how things are so simple to children; even children have a way of getting through to adults with the simplest words or stories.

In order to maintain your why, you cannot make anything about yourself. The why is the reason that keeps you going, but it is also for the greater good. Your why should have you work harder when you're already exhausted and have nothing left. Your why should drive people to you because they see something different in you. Your why should motivate the people that you speak to because they can see your confidence and transparency. When you're being open and honest is when you're being the most helpful to people. Remember you've made it out of your hard times and struggles, and there are people who have no clue on how to do that themselves; they too need the answers or help on how to get out of their situations.

Though our struggles may be temporary, our victories last forever. Learn your why, embrace your why, and show your why with confidence. In this book you've seen how others have lived through their respective trials and overcame them. Our pasts do not define who we are. It just strengthens the people who we are today. Never let anyone tell you that you're not good enough or not worth anything. You are the only one who can tell yourself if you're good enough or not and, even then, you don't have to listen to yourself.

Our struggles make us strong and forgiveness makes us stronger. Use the tools provided in this book to grow your faith, finance, and forgiveness to help better your life and understand your why. When you've discovered your why, you'll discover your happiness on another level.

Acknowledgements

Katie
The ability to forgive changed my life and for that I am forever grateful. I first want to thank God for being the best example of a GIVING and FORGIVING heart. Without God, I would be nothing. I also want to thank my family and friends (my roots) for being a part of my journey and understanding with faith and action, all things are possible. And, finally, I want to thank my Zarvos Leadership and Coaching family. God placed me in Zarvos to help direct my path. It encouraged me to carefully choose my battles and to use my story to help and inspire others. Katie LIVES and so does everyone in my theater. #ThisIsMyRoar #Indy83

Tamesha
First, I would like to thank God, who is truly the head of my life. Without Him, there is no me. I want to thank Him for His love, support, wisdom, and knowledge, and for giving me the ability to serve him wholeheartedly in all that I do; this is a blessing. Second, I would like to thank my family, friends, and mentors for their love and support. Words cannot express how much I appreciate their belief in me, and encouragement to stay focused on my goals and dreams.

Scott
I'd like to thank those who have stood beside me to encourage me along my life's journey. The struggle was real but the blessings have been priceless. When I wrote my first book, "Vision: The Victory Before the Battle", I poured so much of myself into that book to help someone else through my pain and triumph. Never give up on your goals and keep pushing yourself.

Lexi
I'd like to thank God for His goodness and mercy towards me in spite of me. I am thankful for my family, friends, and my four beautiful children, Jade, Marvin, Micah, and Nailah for their support and understanding as I pursue my dreams. Last but not least, I am forever grateful to my financial and business coaches, Todd & Sandra Newkirk and Aprille Franks Hunt. My growth is a direct result of their investment in me.

A portion of the proceeds from this book series goes towards the Nspired Ascensions Inc. Scholarship Fund. If you'd like to contribute to the scholarship fund or make any type of donations please visit our website.

Nspired Ascensions Inc.
www.nspiredascension.com

www.ingramcontent.com/pod-product-compliance
Lightning Source LLC
Chambersburg PA
CBHW060709030426
42337CB00017B/2818